S0-BCP-032

UNDERSTANDING
ADRIENNE KENNEDY

Understanding Contemporary American Literature
Matthew J. Bruccoli, Series Editor

Volumes on

Edward Albee • Sherman Alexie • Nicholson Baker • John Barth
Donald Barthelme • The Beats • The Black Mountain Poets • Robert Bly
Raymond Carver • Fred Chappell • Chicano Literature
Contemporary American Drama
Contemporary American Horror Fiction
Contemporary American Literary Theory
Contemporary American Science Fiction
Contemporary Chicana Literature
Robert Coover • James Dickey • E. L. Doctorow • John Gardner
George Garrett • John Hawkes • Joseph Heller • Lillian Hellman
John Irving • Randall Jarrell • Charles Johnson • Adrienne Kennedy
William Kennedy • Jack Kerouac • Ursula K. Le Guin • Denise Levertov
Bernard Malamud • Bobbie Ann Mason • Jill McCorkle
Carson McCullers • W. S. Merwin • Arthur Miller
Toni Morrison's Fiction • Vladimir Nabokov • Gloria Naylor
Joyce Carol Oates • Tim O'Brien • Flannery O'Connor • Cynthia Ozick
Walker Percy • Katherine Anne Porter • Richard Powers
Reynolds Price • Annie Proulx • Thomas Pynchon
Theodore Roethke • Philip Roth • May Sarton • Hubert Selby, Jr.
Mary Lee Settle • Neil Simon • Isaac Bashevis Singer
Jane Smiley • Gary Snyder • William Stafford • Robert Stone
Anne Tyler • Kurt Vonnegut • David Foster Wallace
Robert Penn Warren • James Welch • Eudora Welty
Tennessee Williams • August Wilson

UNDERSTANDING

ADRIENNE KENNEDY

Philip C. Kolin

University of South Carolina Press

© 2005 University of South Carolina

Published in Columbia, South Carolina, by the
University of South Carolina Press

Manufactured in the United States of America

09   08   07   06   05   5   4   3   2   1

Library of Congress Cataloging-in-Publication Data

Kolin, Philip C.
    Understanding Adrienne Kennedy / Philip C. Kolin.
        p. cm. —   (Understanding contemporary American literature)
    Includes bibliographical references and index.
    ISBN 1-57003-579-2 (cloth : alk. paper)
    1. Kennedy, Adrienne—Criticism and interpretation. 2. Women and
literature—United States—History—20th century. 3. African Americans in literature.   I. Title. II. Series.
    PS3561.E4252Z75 2005
    812'.54—dc22

                                                   2004028469

To Maureen

Contents

Series Editor's Preface

The volumes of *Understanding Contemporary American Literature* have been planned as guides or companions for students as well as good nonacademic readers. The editor and publisher perceive a need for these volumes because much of the influential contemporary literature makes special demands. Uninitiated readers encounter difficulty in approaching works that depart from the traditional forms and techniques of prose and poetry. Literature relies on conventions, but the conventions keep evolving; new writers form their own conventions—which in time may become familiar. Put simply, *UCAL* provides instruction in how to read certain contemporary writers—identifying and explicating their material, themes, use of language, point of view, structures, symbolism, and responses to experience.

The word *understanding* in the titles was deliberately chosen. Many willing readers lack an adequate understanding of how contemporary literature works; that is, what the author is attempting to express and the means by which it is conveyed. Although the criticism and analysis in the series have been aimed at a level of general accessibility, these introductory volumes are meant to be applied in conjunction with the works they cover. They do not provide a substitute for the works and authors they introduce, but rather prepare the reader for more profitable literary experiences.

M. J. B.

Preface

Adrienne Kennedy has been one of the most respected African American playwrights on the American stage for over four decades. Her plays are highly experimental, surrealistic nightmares of young black women (and men) struggling with questions of identity and self-worth in a white, prejudiced world. Radically departing from traditional, sequential plots and consistent characterization, Kennedy's plays stage the harrowing territory of the subconscious, a chaotic world of shifting times, locations, and selves. In fact, Kennedy is most famous for representing her protagonists' fragmentary, conflicting psychological states—their various selves reflected in a host of white, black, and mulatta characters, both historical and imaginary, speaking wildly lyrical, incantatory language on phantasmagoric stages. While Kennedy is not an easy author to read, her challenging works pay rich dividends. Her theater raises profound issues about race, gender, and identity in American culture.

In this book I provide a close reading of fifteen of Kennedy's plays, from her first Obie-winning play, *Funnyhouse of a Negro* (1964), through her various political scripts and *The Alexander Plays* (1992) to *Sleep Deprivation Chamber* (1996) and *June and Jean in Concert* (1996), her latest work to win an Obie. I also give attention to Kennedy's novel *Deadly Triplets: A Theatre Mystery and Journal* (1990) and to some of her short fiction. To help elucidate Kennedy's dramas, I have focused on their complex symbolism, characterization, dramaturgy, and poetry, and especially on her sources, chief of which is her widely honored, unconventional scrapbook-autobiography *People Who Led to My Plays* (1987). Praised for being one of the most personal, confessional dramatists in the American theater, Kennedy has written plays that can only be understood in terms of her family and cultural background, her politics, and even her dreams. The roots of Kennedy's work run deep into African rituals, Christian symbolism, classical mythology, and psychoanalysis, all of which I have brought in at key points to help readers understand and appreciate her visionary, provocative canon.

I would like to thank the administration of the University of Southern Mississippi for granting me a sabbatical leave to work on this book. In particular, I am grateful to Dean Elliott Pood of the College of Arts and Letters for his continuing encouragement and support. My thanks also go to Evelyn Ward of the Cleveland Public Library and to Todd Krispinski of the Great Lakes Theater Festival for their assistance in helping me obtain theater reviews of the Cleveland productions of Kennedy's plays. Tara Wenger at the Harry Ransom Humanities Research Center at the University of Texas at Austin kindly assisted me in obtaining copies of some of Kennedy's early (and unpublished) plays. And I am grateful to Micah Stack for his patience in keyboarding the various drafts from which this book finally evolved.

I am deeply grateful to my children, Kristin, Eric, and Theresa, to my grandchildren, Evan Philip and Megan Elise, and to my extended family of Margie and Al Parish, Deacon Ralph and Mary Torrelli, and Sister Carmelita Stinn, SFCC, for their prayers and love. To my wife Maureen goes my admiration, thanks, and a heart overflowing with love.

UNDERSTANDING
ADRIENNE KENNEDY

CHAPTER 1

Introduction

Adrienne Kennedy and Dreams Noir

For over forty years, Adrienne Kennedy (born Adrienne Lita Hawkins, 13 September 1931) has made major contributions to American theater. Herbert Blau calls her "surely the most original black writer of her generation."[1] Kennedy has won Obies (the equivalent of an Off-Broadway Oscar) for her *Funnyhouse of a Negro* (1964), *June and Jean in Concert* (1995), and *Sleep Deprivation Chamber* (1996). She has become "a fixture of the Off-Broadway scene."[2] Her plays have been staged at such places as La MaMa Experimental Theatre Company, the Theatre Company of Boston, the Goodman Theatre in Chicago, the Julliard School in New York, and the Mark Taper Forum in Los Angeles. Several theaters have devoted a season to her work, including the Great Lakes Theater Festival (1992) in Cleveland and the Signature Company Theatre at the New York Public Theater (1995). Kennedy was the first woman dramatist to have a play—*An Evening with Dead Essex* (1973)—performed at the Yale Repertory Theatre.

Her plays are also highly regarded abroad, having been produced in London at the Royal Court Theatre and at the National Theatre, at the Petit Odeon in Paris, and the San Saba in Rome. Moreover, her dramas have been recorded on Radio Denmark and on the BBC with the Off-Broadway cast and narrated by Emlyn Williams.[3] Kennedy has worked closely with world-famous playwright Edward Albee and producer Joe Papp (who helped launch her career), and with directors Joseph Chaikin, Gerald Freedman, and Michael Kahn and actors Diana Sands, Yaphet Kotto, Ruby Dee, and Robbie McCauley. Finally, her plays have been anthologized frequently; she was one of only five playwrights included in *The Norton Anthology of American Literature* (1989). Also a distinguished mentor, Kennedy has taught at Harvard, Yale, Princeton, the University of California at Berkeley, Brown, Stanford, and elsewhere.

Since the debut of *Funnyhouse of a Negro* in 1964, Kennedy has been on the cutting edge of experimental theater, bringing a unique voice to the African American experience. Departing from the realism of Lorraine Hansberry's *Raisin in the Sun* or the social protest plays of Ed Bullins or Amiri Baraka, Kennedy has written intensely intimate, powerfully nontraditional dramas. Scott Cummings accurately concluded that, in the last forty years, Kennedy has been writing "the most personal plays of any playwright in the U.S.A."[4] Acclaimed as one of the most innovative American playwrights of the twentieth century, she has crafted plays that are interior monologues of young black women caught in surrealistic nightmares. Traumatized by racial oppression, Kennedy's heroines experience identity crises about who they are and where they belong. Perhaps Kennedy's greatest accomplishment has been being one of "the first playwrights to represent the self in multiple characters, an apt metaphor for her experiences as both an African American and a woman in this society."[5] Most of her plays are short, intense jabs to the psyche. They are unsettlingly postmodern —surrealistic, dreamlike, without traditional narrative plots comprising a beginning, middle, and end. Kennedy's works are disturbing, complex, hypnotic. Marc Robinson admits that he "prefers to read them in small doses—a single ten-page play is enough for a sitting."[6]

Yet they offer immense insight into the idea of cultural identity. Kennedy's canon vibrates with the tension and tragedy of what it means to be black in a white world. Her works map the psychological ravages of young black women (and, in some instances, black men) struggling and dying to be seen as white (or to be accepted for who they are) in racist America. But Kennedy has turned her anger at racial prejudice into art. Clive Barnes identified her unique perspective: "Of all our black writers, Kennedy is most concerned with white, with white relationships, with white blood. She thinks black, but she remembers white. It gives her work an eddying ambiguity."[7] Because of the horrors of miscegenation, rape, and racial profiling, her characters are caught in a world gone mad. The funnyhouse, taken from her most famous play, *Funnyhouse of a Negro,* with its characteristic distorting mirrors, is her signature symbol for the madness that surrounds her characters. As Mel Tapley notes, Kennedy's funnyhouse is "this house of America" where bigotry always draws blood.[8] Kennedy mourns discrimination in America in works including *Funnyhouse of a Negro, The Owl Answers, A Rat's Mass, The Ohio State Murders,* and *Sleep Deprivation Chamber.* Her earlier plays are filled with powerful cultural messages as relevant today as they were in the 1960s. In 2003 she won the Lifetime Achievement Award from the Anisfield-Wolf Foundation for works attacking racism.

In more than four decades in the American theater, Kennedy has created a highly diverse canon. Eclecticism is at the heart of her highly charged experimental plays. Her early, breakout works—*Funnyhouse of a Negro, The Owl Answers, A Lesson in Dead Language*—focus on hallucinatory black women. But she has also written several political allegories of black men equally trapped in a racist America—*An Evening with Dead Essex* and *Sun: A Poem for Malcolm X Inspired by His Murder.* In the quartet of her Alexander plays—*She Talks to Beethoven, The Film Club, Dramatic Circle,* and *The Ohio State Murders*—Kennedy fictionalizes herself through writer/lecturer Suzanne Alexander, who recalls events in Kennedy's life from the 1940s through the 1960s. Different in subject matter and technique but not in anger and power from her earlier plays, *Sleep Deprivation Chamber* concentrates on a mother's quest for justice for her victimized son. Kennedy has also adapted the classical Greek tragedies *Orestes* and *Electra* and, in 2001, *Oedipus Rex,* which further reflect her tragic vision of the horrors of contemporary America. Like her plays, these adaptations deal with "the curse of blood." Her love of music has led to *Lancashire Lad* (1980), a musical play commissioned for a children's theater based on the life of Charlie Chaplin. In addition, she collaborated on *The Lennon Play: In His Own Write,* an adaptation of John Lennon's nonsense books, and wrote a libretto for the opera version of *A Rat's Mass.*

Kennedy has also written *Deadly Triplets: A Theatre Mystery and Journal* (1990), an eighty-seven page mystery novel to which she attached a theater journal. Like her plays, Kennedy's novel is highly experimental and confessional. She casts herself as protagonist/persona Suzanne Sand, an aptly named, beautiful playwright of mixed color. Sand becomes embroiled in several murders connected with actors and other theater people as well as the mysterious disappearance and murder of her adoptive British mother thirty years earlier. The twenty-five-page journal, which has been seen as a mirror image of the novel, is filled with sketches of people whom Kennedy actually met while in London between 1966 and 1969, many of whom figure in her novel. In addition to *Deadly Triplets,* she has published numerous short prose pieces, including her early, telling story "Because of the King of France," originally appearing in the journal *Black Orpheus,* about racial identity and prejudice in Louis XIV's court.[9]

To understand Kennedy's plays is to understand her family. As she has repeatedly stressed, "Autobiographical work is the only thing that interests me, apparently because that is what I do best"; her life bleeds into her plays, for "everybody in my family is dramatic."[10] No better guide to Kennedy's family life can be found than her autobiography—*People Who Led to My Plays* (1987), for which she won an American Book Award. One reviewer maintains that *People* is "invaluable for students of a writer for whom the distance between life and art has never been more than a short jump."[11] Ishmael Reed labels *People* as a new type of black autobiography,[12] and, going even further, Caroline Jackson Smith proclaimed that "*People* establishes a whole new genre of autobiography."[13] The book is a combination of memoir, scrapbook, family album, diary, journal, and psychic history covering six periods of Kennedy's life from 1936 to 1961: from "Elementary School, 1936–1943" through junior high, high school, college, marriage and motherhood, and, finally, to "A Voyage, 1960–1961" to Africa. Kennedy says the publisher even made *People* look like her mother's red photograph album.[14]

People is an unconventional and, chronologically, very freely organized book. "Rather than employing a traditional narrative structure, Kennedy . . . [offers] a collection of images and short descriptions, bits of remembered dialogue, feelings, events, and yearnings evoked by the memory of significant people in her life."[15] It includes short entries not only on people, including "Myself," but also on places, images, books, films, and events that would become the building blocks for Kennedy's plays. Written in the first person, *People* reveals Kennedy's most intimate thoughts and dreams. She has said that the "characters are myself."[16] From the start, *People* touches upon Kennedy's school and church, where spirituals and images of Jesus seized her imagination, as well as the myriad banquets, associations, individuals, and occasions that have shaped her art. Illustrating the diverse influences on Kennedy's childhood, adolescent, and early adult years are numerous photos, drawings, artworks, newspaper clippings, and even religious cards scattered across the pages of *People*.

Most penetratingly, however, *People* documents the extensive influence film had on the young Kennedy and her work. Alongside photos of her family are pictures of movie stars Bette Davis (Kennedy's favorite), Elizabeth Taylor, Jean Peters, and Marlon Brando (all of whom appear in her *A Movie Star Has to Star in Black and White*), as well as Clark Gable, Ingrid Bergman, Shelley Winters, Gene Kelly, and others. These glamorous stars, showcased in the photographs, would play a major role in the visual politics of whiteness and blackness at the heart of Kennedy's plays. Keeping "*Modern Screen* in [her] vanity table" (*People,* 41) and devouring *Glamour* magazine, Kennedy became a vicarious participant in Hollywood fictions. The movies encouraged her desire for beauty, fame, and love, the dreams that capture so many of her protagonists. She claimed the stars as her "extended family" and even wanted to be a "forties movie star" herself.[17] Speaking of her junior-high-school impressions of the "heroines" in Bette Davis's movies, Kennedy exalted: "They dressed so beautifully and were adored by men.

I wanted to be like that" (47). In high school, she went to French film festivals, even though she did not know the language.

Yet, hauntingly, *People* also includes photographs of Dracula, the Wolf Man, and Frankenstein, as well as references to monsters, ghosts, vampires, and ghouls, together with her scrapbook pictures of beautiful Hollywood stars, foreshadowing how, in Kennedy's imagination, romantic dreams can turn into howling nightmares. Kennedy recalls, "Because of the Wolf Man I asked my mother many questions about what happens to 'a person' while sleeping" (16). Kennedy was as fascinated by the glamorous as she was by the horrific, a contrast emphasized in so many of her plays with such frequency that they have been seen as highly cinematic. In fact, Kennedy herself was asked to write a "screenplay" of her life "as a Black woman" living in London in the late 1960s, but she "declined" (*Deadly Triplets*, 99).

Other influences on her work documented in *People* include music (particularly Beethoven), history, and art, especially the works of Van Gogh, whose self-portrait looms forebodingly above a photograph of Dizzy Gillespie and a painting of Queen Elizabeth I on a single page. Kennedy was enthralled by such black artists as Louis Armstrong, Charlie Mingus, Count Basie, Duke Ellington, and Miles Davis, whom she termed "Inspiration!" (*People*, 87). In school, she excelled in the classics, studying Virgil, and joined the Latin club, learning experiences possibly echoed in her *A Lesson in Dead Language*. Seeing herself as an aspiring writer, she kept journals and diaries, wrote stories, submitted fiction to *Seventeen* magazine, and went to plays at the old Palace Theatre in Cleveland as well as concerts, including a special one by Paul Robeson. She also read deeply from the works of black authors. Of James Baldwin she said: "He sharpened my entire vision of America" (99).

But when Kennedy saw Tennessee Williams's *The Glass Menagerie* in high school, she recalled "the idea of being a writer and seeing my family on stage caught fire in my mind" (61). In the 1950s, she worked on several scripts that imitated Williams, most notably her early, unpublished play *Pale Blue Flowers* (1955), where a young man named Maurice tells his companions, "the three of us can leave for my wilderness" by following his imaginative flights. But his more realistic friend shoots him down: "Put your toy trunk away, Tom Sawyer. Your explorations are dreams."[18] Kennedy later moved far from Williams's theater filled with deeply mythological plots and romantic characters. She confesses in *People,* "It took me ten years to stop imitating him, to stop using his form and to stop stealing his themes, which were not mine" (94). Even so, looking back at the 1950s, Kennedy admitted, "It had been a long time since I had thought of Williams, but now [1961], as I stood staring at volumes of *Streetcar, The Glass Menagerie,* and *The Rose Tattoo,* I realized how much I still admired what he did."[19]

Above all else, *People* is an album, a scrapbook of memories, in words and pictures, of the family life and traumas she would put on stage. Kennedy was raised in Cleveland, Ohio, but her family roots were in Montezuma, Georgia, a small town in southwest Georgia that had a 70 percent black population and a 30 percent white one (22). These two locations—one the urban North and the other the agrarian South—have provided highly symbolic psychic landscapes for her works. In 1930s and 1940s Cleveland she lived in the integrated, multiethnic neighborhoods of Mount Pleasant and Glenville, a biographical fact that must be given great emphasis in the context of the racial tensions and identities explored in her plays. Kennedy points out: "It is important to remember I grew up in an immigrant

neighborhood but was the product of black middle-class culture, and I always tried to make sense of that, tried to balance
that. To understand where I fit into that world."[20]

At first, the balancing was easier. Kennedy's Cleveland
neighborhood of Mount Pleasant had about 60 percent Italian
residents; others had come from Eastern Europe and Ireland.
The neighborhood also drew African Americans who flocked
to this northern city as a refuge from oppression and for eco-
nomic opportunities. Kennedy and her younger brother Cornell
claimed many childhood friends among the Italian families in
their neighborhood, and they witnessed a variety of faith prac-
tices, especially from Roman Catholicism and Judaism. Ironically, many of Kennedy's heroines tragically search for identity
among and are rejected by the cultural institutions of white religion that were a part of her Cleveland childhood, an overriding
theme in her plays. An Italian girl, Rosemary, damns the black
children in *A Rat's Mass*. The boyfriend who mocks *Funnyhouse of a Negro*'s Sarah is a Jewish poet named Raymond;
coincidentally a young black boy, Sidney, one of the narrator's
distant cousins in "Because of the King of France," falls in love
at the age of sixteen with a Jewish girl, Sylvia Klein, whom he
gets pregnant and whose father "beat [him] with a lead pipe."
Sidney's mother admonishes him, "It's the Lord's will you're
black and she's white."[21]

Every summer for over ten years of her childhood, Kennedy
and her brother traveled from Cleveland in Jim Crow train cars
to visit their grandmother and extended family of aunts, uncles,
and cousins in segregated Montezuma. Significant in terms of
Kennedy's own mulatta heroines, she also visited her maternal
grandfather, a wealthy white man who owned peach orchards.[22]
In *Deadly Triplets,* Kennedy disclosed through Suzanne Sand,

her persona, that "long ago my mother had told me her father's family came from England" (106). Though the fact is not mentioned in *People,* Kennedy's mixed racial heritage may help to explain the struggles of her mulatta heroines. In Montezuma, she fantasized that since so many black residents had white ancestors who were descended from England that she, too, could trace her lineage to Anglo-Saxon stock, as her heroine Clara Passmore does in *The Owl Answers* and Brother and Sister attempt to do in *A Rat's Mass*. Kennedy confesses, "I've seemingly only been successful in creating these heroines who are very close variations of me, and I'm not necessarily able to understand it."[23]

Unquestionably the strongest early influences on Kennedy were her parents, who left her an invaluable legacy that she wove into the fabric of her plays. "I'm very much my parents' child still, and so a lot of what I write is about their lives," she told Cal Wilson.[24] Her parents appear as characters in *June and Jean in Concert* (1995), a dramatization of *People Who Led to My Plays,* and in many other ways in her canon. Kennedy's father, Cornell Wallace Hawkins, called C. W., was a social worker and an executive secretary for the YMCA's Cedar branch in Cleveland. A passionately political man, C. W. strove to advance the cause of black people in the 1930s and 1940s. He eventually became the Assistant Head of Race Relations at Cleveland City Hall. Both of her parents, in fact, "had a tremendous feeling about helping blacks," Kennedy said.[25] In a later interview, she proudly affirmed, "I grew up in a home where people wrote and were members of the NAACP and the United Negro College Fund. I knew my alliances."[26]

Her father, a graduate of Morehouse College, was frequently cited in the newspapers for his spirited speeches espousing the NAACP. "He had the same cadence in his voice as Martin Luther King," Kennedy later recalled, and "his speeches were in biblical and social work tones."[27] She absorbed her father's opinions about major black leaders and the needs of the black community and fondly remembers his reading to her from works by Langston Hughes and James Weldon Johnson, the author of the highly influential African American novel *The Autobiography of an Ex-Colored Man* (1912). Issues of *Crisis,* the official magazine of the NAACP, were often on her father's desk filled with outrages against blacks (lynchings, segregation) and calls for more militant action to win black freedom and power. *People* tells how C.W. wanted his daughter to be a "great woman" like Eleanor Roosevelt, Marion Anderson, the black singer who brought Washington, D.C., to tears with her rendition of the National Anthem, or Mary Bethune, the black educator. He died in 1975.

The dreams and fears of the black community, as reflected in her father's speeches and activities, indelibly shaped Kennedy's work. *An Evening with Dead Essex* is about Mark Essex, a young black sniper shot down by New Orleans police; Malcolm X is the focus of her *Sun;* and her *Black Children's Day,* about the history of blacks in Rhode Island, was commissioned by the Rites and Reason program at Brown University. *Sleep Deprivation Chamber* (1996), the surrealistic documentary about how her own son Adam was victimized by police brutality, glows with the same indignation that Kennedy heard in her father's speeches. In fact, *Sleep Deprivation Chamber* is interwoven with dream sequences of prejudices in the 1940s paralleling those of the 1990s. Earlier, in *Funnyhouse of a Negro,* she had presented a bloodied Patrice Lumumba, the black nationalist premier of the Congo who was brutally assassinated, and in *People* Kennedy admitted that "there was no doubt that Lumumba, this murdered hero, was merged in my mind with my father" (119–20).

But while Kennedy's plays and her continuing rage at prejudice certainly should be viewed in the context of her father's political speeches, she compellingly transformed his politics of race into the performance of self, replacing didactic political agendas with traumatic interior monologues by black heroines engulfed in hallucinations because of hatred by a white world. Misleadingly, in the 1960s, Kennedy's plays were criticized by some as "irrelevant" because they were not seen as promoting black pride.[28] But beyond doubt, Kennedy has launched her own black revolution, which took her in a different direction. Rather than intoning "Lift Every Voice and Sing," the James Weldon Johnson song regarded as the black national anthem by her father's generation, Kennedy recalled that "it seemed that we as 'Negroes' sang of sorrow," thinking of her cousins in a Georgia church or even her mother cooking "Sunday-morning breakfast" (97). Like the spirituals her family sang, Kennedy's plays mourn the tragedies of black women—really, all vulnerable women—who are cast into a nightmare world because of racial or gender stereotyping.

Kennedy credits her mother, Etta Haugabook Hawkins, for the inspiration to write plays that evolved from dreams. Not going to work as a fifth-grade science teacher until Kennedy was eleven, her mother taught her to read at age three. Kennedy lovingly recalls, "I was totally my mother's confidante."[29] Her mother encouraged her to be fiercely competitive, excelling in every school activity, a pressure that Kennedy says marks her still. Speaking for Kennedy, the character Jean writes in her diary that when she and her sister June were introduced to Dr. Benjamin Mays, president of Morehouse College, by their parents: "We wanted him to know we were prodigies" (*June and Jean in Concert,* 245). Beyond exhorting Kennedy to discipline and excellence, her mother's stories shaped both the form and the content of many of her plays. As she told playwright Suzan-Lori Parks, "My mother always talked to me. She would tell things that happened to her . . . her dreams, her past . . . it's like the monologues in my plays, it really is. Because her stories were loaded with imagery and tragedy of darkness and sarcasm . . . and humor. She could describe a day when she was sitting on her porch in Georgia and what happened."[30] Kennedy further revealed that her plays "have the same tone as [my] mother's stories."[31] In *People,* the playwright recorded her desire to learn more from her mother's dreams. "When my mother was making oatmeal on winter mornings, I sat waiting with my bowl at the kitchen table, I secretly yearned that my mother would talk *more* about the people she had dreamed about. There is no doubt that a person talking about the people in his or her dreams became an archetype for the people in my monologues, plays, and stories" (33). Reinforcing the point later, Kennedy shows twin daughters anxiously waiting to hear their mother's dreams in *June and Jean in Concert.*

Through her mother and her circle of socially conscious friends, Kennedy also learned about their sophisticated tastes in clothes, books, movies, and music, as well as about the issues in general affecting the black community, all of which powerfully encouraged her to emulate these beautiful women. She recalls listening to her mother's friends proudly talking about Lena Horne, the only black star in Hollywood in the 1940s, or enjoying their conversations about Billie Holiday's enchanted voice and beauty. But there was a negative side of childhood for Kennedy, which also influenced her later work. "I wasn't allowed to express what I was thinking. I had to say things that were correct in school and at home. So all these people were burning inside of me."[32] She experienced the same pain as Zora Neale Hurston, who claimed, "There is no agony like bearing an untold story."[33] Kennedy internalized and transformed the untold stories of her mother and her mother's sensitive and accomplished friends (as well as her own) in creating forlorn heroines such as Sarah in *Funnyhouse of a Negro*, Clara in *The Owl Answers,* or young Suzanne in *The Ohio State Murders.*

Kennedy learned about racial injustice from her mother as she did from her social-worker father. "My mother was quite violent in her language as I grew up feeling blacks were hated people."[34] When Kennedy attended Ohio State University (1949–1953), where she graduated with a degree in elementary education, she realized firsthand how threatening to self and family racial prejudice could be. Protected by a loving black community and growing up in racially diverse neighborhoods, Kennedy was not ready for the real-life rejection that prejudice could unleash (blacks at Ohio State could not join clubs or major in English), or the unspeakable tragedies it would lead to in her work—the child killing of *The Ohio State Murders* or the brutalities in *Sleep Deprivation Chamber.*

Shortly after graduation from Ohio State, Kennedy married Joseph Kennedy, who, like Clara's husband Eddie in *Movie Star,* went off to war in Korea. Returning from Korea, he moved his family to New York City (the place where Kennedy says she is most comfortable writing) and worked on his Ph.D. at Columbia University while she took writing classes, imitating Tennessee Williams and others, but with no promise of publication of her work. Though she and Joseph were divorced after thirteen years of marriage, Kennedy acknowledges his encouraging her as a writer. He "released me from this image of myself as simply somebody to teach second grade."[35] After he graduated, her husband took a job with the African Research Foundation and gave Kennedy the single most important opportunity of her career. When she was twenty-nine, she accompanied him to Africa where she and her work underwent an epiphanic change. As she tells Kathleen Betsko and Rachel Koenig, "In the 14 months I was out of the country, my writing became sharper, more focused, powerful and less imitative."[36]

Moving away from the realistic/naturalistic dramatic conventions and characterizations she found in the authors she had been imitating, Kennedy embraced "the strength in being a black person and a connection to West Africa."[37] She learned and adopted incantatory African rituals and drama, masks, songs, and poetry, and discovered a radical, new way of representing character, all of which led to her first professional successes—*Funnyhouse of a Negro* and *The Owl Answers*. Reflecting on her early career, Kennedy acknowledges the help and support she received from her family. "I was surrounded by people who were encouraging of me and that coupled with my rage—not only at Ohio State but my rage about race in general—the combination has paid off."[38] The people who led to her plays became voices in them.

Kennedy's themes emerge from the shaping influence of her father's speeches, her mother's stories and dreams, and her own poignant experiences in Africa. Race, identity, gender, family, and nightmares converge in her plays as mutually inclusive themes. She admits in the preface to *Deadly Triplets* that her plays are "filled with the intricacies of race in my life" (viii). The overriding message in Kennedy's canon might be summed up in Sarah's plight in *Funnyhouse of a Negro*: "She is lost in a nightmare world where black is evil and white is good." Deconstructing white/black polarities, Kennedy concentrates on the conflicting cultural identities embedded in whiteness/blackness that were the subject of much discussion for generations. In the 1920s, the black cultural historian and critic W. E. B. DuBois praised "the Negro" for a "double consciousness, this sense of always looking at one's self through the eyes of others, of measuring one's soul by a . . . world that looks on in amused contempt and pity." But while DuBois honored the "American Negro" for this "two-ness," his or her "two souls, two thoughts, two unreconciled strivings, two warring ideals in one dark body, whose dogged strength alone keeps it from being torn asunder,"[39] Kennedy's heroines are not strengthened because of their "two-ness" but in fact are torn apart by paranoia, schizophrenia, and death as a result of it.

In some plays, Kennedy focuses on black characters who fantasize about being white—e.g., Clara in *Movie Star*—but are victimized for their desires. In other plays, she choreographs women condemned by miscegenation for being half black and half white—the mulatta Sarah in *Funnyhouse of a Negro,* Clara Passmore in *The Owl Answers,* or Suzanne's kidnapped babies in *The Ohio State Murders*—and who do not fit in and are destroyed by violence. In still other plays—*A Lesson in Dead Language* or *June and Jean in Concert*—Kennedy emphasizes the rite of sexual passage for black girls through violence, family deaths, and nightmares. Suzan-Lori Parks movingly expressed one of the greatest tragedies in Kennedy's plays—that is, "to fall in love with something that didn't include you."[40]

During the 1960s race was often seen as the dominant theme in Kennedy's canon. But the plight of her protagonists was subsequently enlarged and explored through the perspective of feminist studies.[41] Racial crimes and offenses in her work have also raised key gender issues, such as women's roles, identities, and rights in society; the oppression of daughters and wives; and the cultural representations of a woman's body. Speaking for Kennedy, Suzanne Sand in *Deadly Triplets* reveals that a new play she wrote for the Public Theater in New York "seems to possess the mystery and intrigue of unresolved identity that seems to permeate my work" (76). Bewailing the trauma of "unresolved identity," Kennedy's plays explore gender itself as a performance as they emphasize a woman's tragedy. Yet it is not just her tragic protagonists who go through a nightmare; it devastates a family, a generation, a nation. Kennedy's adaptations of Greek plays on Orestes, Oedipus, and Electra also continue her exploration of family tragedies or nightmares leading to the death of children, a recurrent theme in Kennedy's work from *A Rat's Mass* (1963) to *The Ohio State Murders* (1992) and beyond. The American dream has turned into the American nightmare for the extended family of Kennedy's heroines.

Kennedy's dramatic techniques may have originated in her mother's dreams but they have flourished in hers. She kept "loads of notebooks with images, dreams, ideas I've jotted down."[42] In an entry on "Jung" in *People* during the period "Marriage and Motherhood, 1953–1960," the prelude years to *Funnyhouse of a Negro,* Kennedy chided herself, "Dreams, memories. I must stop trying to ignore them" (95). And she didn't. *A Rat's Mass* is based on a dream she had of being "pursued by bloody rats." In that play, her stage captures the horrors of rats everywhere—in the rafters of the house where the play is set, in the characters who have rat heads and tails, and even in the sounds of rats gnawing. Reading a Kennedy play, in fact, is like living in a nightmare. It is a haunting, frightening experience—we enter a world of shadows, unrealities. Like a nightmare, everything in Kennedy's plays is disjointed, distorted, terrifying. Using expressionistic techniques—through music, sound, sight, movement, props to express subconscious states —her plays are horrifying spectacles, a theater of hysteria.

If Kennedy's stagecraft is terrifying, so is the representation of her characters. Many of them look grotesque; they wear black masks or are "*Negroes with painted white faces.*" As in *A Rat's Mass*, people turn into animals—owls, large white dogs, beasts. Shrieks, howls, and cries accompany their grueling acts of harrowing proportion such as murders, heads split apart, babies slain, girls dripping in blood, all ritualistic horrors. Characters are chased, hounded, abused, beaten, imprisoned, machine-gunned as if in a nightmare. Time and place shift constantly for them. Chronology falls apart. Jesus joins Queen Victoria and Patrice Lumumba in *Funnyhouse of a Negro*. In *The Ohio State Murders*, Suzanne Alexander lectures on and relives a nightmare she had experienced forty years ago, but her story defies the logic of chronology. Audiences learn who the murderer of her children is before the murder is committed in Suzanne's play.

Kennedy's nightmarish stagecraft was doubtless influenced by and combines elements from film noir, most often associated with crime films. In fact, because of their affinity to film noir, Kennedy's plays might be called dreams noir. The film noir genre includes such classics of the 1940s and 1950s (Kennedy's artistic gestation period) as *This Gun for Hire* (1942), *Murder, My Sweet* (1944), *Mildred Pierce* (1945), which Kennedy cites in *People*, and *The Lady from Shanghai* (1948). The last-named film concludes with a scene in a theater with a hall of mirrors on stage much like the Cleveland amusement park Kennedy visited, which served as a source for *Funnyhouse of a Negro*.[43] *A Rat's Mass*, *Funnyhouse of a Negro*, *The Owl Answers*, *A Beast*

Story, and surely *The Ohio State Murders* and *Motherhood 2000,* too, incorporate many of the situations and techniques of film noir. Kennedy's plays, like scenes in film noir, take place at night in the shadows; they are full of corpses—victims of bloody crime, especially crimes of passion. Her characters, again like those in film noir, experience "paranoia and entrapment," doomed victims of *"l'amour fatal."*[44] As film noir characteristically did, Kennedy's plays also include flashbacks, blackouts, dissolves, voice-overs, all of which heighten their nightmarish, ghoulish quality.

Using the sights and sounds of nightmares—or dreams noir —Kennedy creates her characters from the inside out. Her theater explores the interior worlds of young, tormented black women—their fantasies and their fears. She describes her plays as "states of mind," and the tortured states of mind in which her characters live emerge again from Kennedy's own experiences: "I feel overwhelmed by family problems and family realities. I see my writing as an outlet for inner, psychological confusion and questions stemming from childhood."[45] In representing their internal confusions, Kennedy departs from the traditional concept of characters as single, realistic entities—coherent, consistent, and knowable. Instead, her characters are fragmented, splintered, often dispersed into warring selves. They are dispossessed persons caught in the flux of rapidly shifting, alternating identities, all inside their own skin. In *The Owl Answers,* for example, Clara is a young black teacher "who is the Virgin Mary who is the Bastard who is the Owl," all at the same time; aspects of Sarah's various selves in *Funnyhouse of a Negro* are divided among the Duchess of Hapsburg, Queen Victoria, Patrice Lumumba, and even Jesus; in *Movie Star,* Clara's life is played by three sets of movie stars through whom she leads her life and who speak her lines. Even in Kennedy's later Alexander play *The Ohio State Murders,* character exists as dyads—an older Suzanne announces and analyzes what her younger self says and does on a stage before or alongside her.

Clinically speaking, Kennedy's traumatized heroines exhibit a condition that psychiatrists have labeled a "dissociative identity disorder," or a "disturbance in identity whereby two or more separate personalities or identities, known as alters, control an individual's behavior."[46] As in Kennedy's plays, these "alters . . . may exhibit different behaviors, mannerisms, personalities, gender orientation, and physical properties."[47] The alters in Kennedy's theater can indict and threaten protagonists, as Shakespeare and Chaucer do to the mulatta Clara in *The Owl Answers,* or mock ominously, as the Duchess of Hapsburg and Queen Victoria do to Sarah in *Funnyhouse of a Negro.* Historical figures—who often represent one or more of a heroine's selves—frequently exist alongside characters emerging from a heroine's past.

Victimized by a severe childhood trauma, individuals with dissociative identity disorder exhibit symptoms curiously similar to the behavior of Kennedy's protagonists—hallucinations, identity confusion and alteration, night terrors, flashbacks, and especially "compulsions and rituals." Most of all, they experience hopelessness.[48] In *Funnyhouse of a Negro, The Owl Answers,* and *A Lesson in Dead Language,* for instance, Kennedy's young heroines go through a series of incantatory refrains and chants and repeat traumatic, bloody events as in a ritual. They retell bits and pieces of their psychic biographies and relive the tortures that break them apart. Characters in Kennedy's plays never reach a catharsis; their psychic wounds just bleed, and bleed. In her later plays, characters go through a different set of rituals and flashbacks. In no way a hallucinatory character, Suzanne Alexander in *The Ohio State Murders* lives through the agonizing process of identifying her children's murderer. In *Sleep Deprivation Chamber*—a perfect title for night terrors!—hard-pounding courtroom rituals (documentary testimony and rebuttals) alternate with dream sequences of Suzanne as a young girl in 1943 Cleveland or at college in 1961.

The rooms Kennedy's characters inhabit are like their minds. As in a nightmare, place is not stable, orderly, or even known or recognizable, because space in Kennedy's plays is not physical; it represents her characters' hallucinations. Rooms for Kennedy never enlarge, never fill up with sunlight. They are claustrophobic torture chambers. Living in their interior worlds, her characters are condemned to walk on physical sets symbolizing their alienation, panic, and madness—funnyhouses, rat-infested churches, the Tower of London, intimidating courtrooms, death-deep ravines. A Kennedy set can simultaneously represent multiple, interconnected, and shifting locations. For instance, *The Owl Answers* takes place in a subway that turns first into the Tower of London, next into St. Peter's in Rome, and then into a seedy Harlem hotel room, before turning back into each locale again. Each of these sets symbolizes an occasion for Clara's punishments for being black. In *Funnyhouse of a Negro,* Sarah lives in a room full of cruel mirrors transporting her to London, Africa, and back to the Upper West Side of New York to counterpoint her self-loathing. In *A Lesson in Dead Language,* a classroom turns into a prison where nativity figures are transformed into a firing squad of Nazis. Setting becomes a scary netherworld in Kennedy's plays.

Consistent with her surrealistic staging, Kennedy's violent symbolism and verbal imagery are signature features of her works, and one major reason for her success as an experimental playwright. She has written "extraordinary short dramas, compounded by poetry, terror, and wit."[49] Kennedy, who claims her plays are "abstract poems,"[50] was heavily influenced by symbolist poets and playwrights such as Federico García Lorca and Tennessee Williams. In each of her plays, heterogeneous symbols and images are yoked together by violence. Severed limbs, wounded heads, festering sores, and blood are everywhere, verbally in the script and physically on stage. "I just have this thing about blood,"[51] admits Kennedy. The black/white imagery in her plays is complemented by black/white props and costuming, e.g., a pale white statue of Queen Victoria in *Funnyhouse of a Negro,* a rich white man wearing a mask to conceal a black pastor in *The Owl Answers.*

Kennedy draws much of her imagery and some of her sets from biblical sources. Although her plays are heavily indebted to the Psalms,[52] they seem also to have apocalyptic roots. A zoo of loathsome beasts populate her scripts—noxious owls, swooping ravens, rats, a grotesque, speaking white dog. *A Beast Story* reads like a prophecy from Revelations on stage. But Kennedy repeatedly shows how Christian images and symbols have been perverted by a racist society—for example, the bloody sacrificial altar in *The Owl Answers,* a cross for the crucifixion in *Motherhood 2000,* a nativity scene and the Eucharist in *A Lesson in Dead Language,* or the altar and aisle for the sacrilegious rituals in *A Rat's Mass.* Yet, paradoxically, her plays are hauntingly lyrical, containing refrains of fuguelike beauty. For example, in *Funnyhouse of a Negro,* a poetic litany about "golden savannas, nim and white frankopenny trees and white stallions roaming under a blue sky" recurs at key psychological moments in Sarah's tragedy, illuminating Kennedy's own African odyssey on stage. Kennedy's plays, then, combine acts of grotesque violence with nightmarish sets and powerful poetic rituals.

CHAPTER 2

A War of Selves in
Funnyhouse of a Negro

Funnyhouse of a Negro is Kennedy's first performed and best-known work. This play, as well as the six others that followed it, launched her career; all seven were produced by 1969. With *Funnyhouse of a Negro,* Kennedy discovered her unique voice and surrealistic style. She began writing the play in 1960 and 1961 in West Africa and continued to work on it in Rome after her mind-changing trip to Ghana and Nigeria with her husband. As she revealed in *People,* "We sailed back to New York on the *United States.* I had a completed play in my suitcase. How could I know it would establish me as a playwright and change my life? After years of writing, I had finally written of myself and my family and it would be on stage and in a book too" (*People,* 125).

Edward Albee, the three-time Pulitzer Prize–winning dramatist and author of *Who's Afraid of Virginia Woolf?* (1962), played a key role in Kennedy's career as her mentor and first producer. In January 1962, he accepted Kennedy into his nonprofit Playwrights' Workshop; as a part of her workshop experience, *Funnyhouse of a Negro* was staged Off Broadway at the Circle in the Square Theatre in 1963, starring Yaphet Kotto as Lumumba and Diana Sands as Sarah. Initially, though, Kennedy wanted to withdraw her manuscript, fearful that it revealed too many intimate details about herself. "I decided to drop out of the class," she confessed. But a resolute Albee replied, "It's your decision. But don't you want to see your play performed? It is a chance to see your characters on stage." Finding Albee "hypnotic," Kennedy recalled his lecturing, "Do you know what a playwright is? A playwright is someone who lets his guts out on the stage, and that is what you've done in this play."[1] Albee persuaded Kennedy to allow her play to be produced, and so *Funnyhouse of a Negro* joined the ranks of major American dramas of the twentieth century. Adrienne Kennedy had begun her long career of writing gut-wrenching plays.

Albee's production company (including Albee, Richard Barr and Clinton Wilder) sponsored the first professional production of *Funnyhouse of a Negro* at the East End Theatre, where it opened on 14 January 1964, for thirty-four performances. This production starred Billie Allen as the Negro Sarah, Cynthia Belgrave as Queen Victoria, Ellen Holly as the Duchess of Hapsburg, Gus Williams as Patrice Lumumba, and Norman Bush as Jesus, and was directed by Michael Kahn. Kennedy had continued working on *Funnyhouse of a Negro* with Kahn since the earlier workshop production. Appropriately, William Ritman, who designed the sets for Albee's *Who's Afraid of Virginia Woolf?* and *Tiny Alice,* was responsible for the premiere of *Funnyhouse of a Negro,* creating a set that was "just twisted enough" for one critic and "all askew" for another.[2] Kennedy won her first Obie for *Funnyhouse of a Negro* in 1965, and later recorded her gratitude to Albee in the acknowledgments to *People Who Led to My Plays.* Financially and creatively, then, Kennedy was closely associated with Albee in the early 1960s, as was another black playwright, LeRoi Jones (later Amiri Baraka), whose *Dutchman* Albee had also sponsored.

Emphasizing Albee's pervasive influence on her career, Kennedy recalled in a 1977 interview:

I first had my plays done in the early sixties and, as a result, I'm really a product of that time when *Zoo Story* and *American Dream* were the models of success. I studied with Edward Albee at one point, just after I had written *Funnyhouse of a Negro*. I would never have even gone for the one-act, except for the fact that everyone was going to see *Zoo Story* and because I was not happy with any of the three-acts I had written up to that point. I couldn't seem to sustain the power and still can't seem to write really long, huge works.[3]

Funnyhouse of a Negro was unquestionably a "product of that time" when Albee's own breakout one-act play *The Zoo Story* (1959; 1960) changed the direction of the American theater with its radical antihero, beatnik Jerry, and his messages of alienation, absurdity, and confrontation. Like Albee's *The Zoo Story* and *The American Dream, Funnyhouse of a Negro* belonged to a revolutionary and highly experimental decade. Kennedy's play grew out of the turbulent early 1960s with its bloodshed over civil rights, the assassination of President John F. Kennedy in 1963, the Watts riots in Los Angeles in 1965, and the looming holocaust of the Vietnam War. As *The American Dream* and *Who's Afraid of Virginia Woolf?* did, *Funnyhouse of a Negro* testified to an American culture of violence. Like Albee, Kennedy bravely brought taboo subjects into the theater. *Funnyhouse of a Negro* explored incest, miscegenation, racial genocide, and female oppression years before they would be freely staged elsewhere. The year *Funnyhouse of a Negro* premiered, for example, saw the arrival of the television version of *Peyton Place,* which, by comparison, dealt with far less shocking subjects such as adultery and drunkenness. Most important, though, Kennedy, like Albee, bolted from the conventions of realistic/naturalistic theater. But she went far beyond the

influence of a European theater of the absurd, which inspired
Albee's early plays, to combine surrealistic techniques with the
rituals and rhythms of the African culture she had witnessed
firsthand in 1961 in Ghana.

The protagonist of *Funnyhouse of a Negro*—the Negro
Sarah—is the first in a long line of Kennedy's hallucinatory
heroines. She lives in a terrifying world of nightmares, wild
flights of hysteria, and incantatory laments. When she first
appears, "*She is a faceless, dark character with a hangman's
rope around her neck and red blood on the part that would be
her face*" (13). This emblem symbolizes her despair and prefigures her tragic suicide at the play's conclusion. Throughout her
long, confessional monologues, which flow tragically from her
red, bloodied mouth, Sarah through her various selves cries out,
"I want not to be," and then reveals the source of her hopelessness. Because of her mixed racial heritage, she becomes a "child
of torment" (17). Her black father, "the darkest of us all," has
"haunted my conception, diseased my birth" (13). She fantasizes that her own mother, "fairest of them all," "looked like a
white woman" (12), with straight hair. Driven to an asylum
because of the horror of being raped by a black man, Sarah's
mother "comb[ed] her straight black hair and wove long dreams
of her beauty" (20)—evoking the mad Ophelia in *Hamlet*.
"Trapped in blackness," Sarah's mother is both victim and
accuser. She drifts in and out of the play "*dressed in a white
nightgown . . . carrying before her a bald head. She moves as
one in a trance . . . Her hair is wild, straight, and black and falls
to her waist*" (11), all horrifying reminders of the consequences
of Sarah's black ancestry.

As the product of this unholy union, Sarah is ridden with
guilt and shame. "I betrayed my mother," (21) she confesses,
by being a child of a dark race whose collective soul she finds

stained. With self-loathing, Sarah declares that her mother "saw I was a black man's child and she preferred speaking to owls" (20), that is, she seeks refuge in a secret world that transcends the crime and frees her from daily contact with either her husband or Sarah. The owl, though, conveys other racially symbolic meanings that Kennedy developed more fully in *The Owl Answers*. Ironically, the owl is an ominous symbol of the tragic yellow mulatta, Sarah, "the child of torment who is neither white nor black." As Sarah's black father declares, "I created a yellow child who hates me" (21). Sarah, the yellow mulatta, lives in trauma because of the contradictions and dichotomies in her life that she can neither reconcile nor assimilate. As Howard Taubman asserted, Kennedy's play "digs into the tormented mind of a Negro who cannot bear the burden of being a Negro and [is] too proud to accept patronage of the white world."[4] Wanting to be white but looking black, with her kinky, frizzy hair, Sarah does not fit neatly into the white world. Instead, she inhabits a harrowing, liminal world where she slips into madness. In her own mind, she is condemned to fantasize the worst horrors about her conflicting racial heritage. In hallucinating about her dysfunctional family, she turns her father into a "wild black beast" (13), a rapist from an encroaching jungle, and her mother into a specter who, paradoxically, also haunts the memory of Sarah's nativity.

Hair and skin color—among the two most prominent cultural signifiers of race—become the leading tropes in Kennedy's plays. "I have a thing for hair," she has confessed. In *Funnyhouse of a Negro* in particular, hair plays an immense role in Sarah's tragedy, as Kennedy explores its many nuances, psychologically and politically. Hair becomes linked to self-recognition and self-contempt. The various references to and representations of wild, kinky hair symbolize Sarah's own frenzied state, her confusion of being. For Sarah, kinky hair stigmatizes her as the outcast Negro. In contrast, when Kennedy was making a positive connection to her African heritage, she recalled that on her trip to Ghana "this was the first time in my life that it was impossible to keep my hair straightened. In Ghana and for the rest of the thirteen month trip I stopped straightening my hair."[5]

Significantly, every major character in *Funnyhouse of a Negro* suffers from having his or her hair fall out, acts graphically presented on stage. As punishment for being raped by a black man, Sarah's mother ends up being "in the asylum bald" (18). Sarah, too, loses her hair because she "wavered in her opinion" of her self as a white person (14). "*A patch of hair*" is "*missing from the crown which the Negro carries in her hand*" (13). The characters who represent Sarah's white selves, the Duchess of Hapsburg and Queen Victoria, lose their hair as well. Oppressed by her blackness, the Duchess "*screams and opens her red paper bag and draws from it her fallen hair. It is a great mass of dark wild hair*" (17). Similarly, Queen Victoria's "*white gown is covered with fallen out hair,*" which is also strewn "*on her pillow*" (18), symbolizing that her whiteness is endangered and stained by contact with negritude. Patrice Lumumba, or the Black Man, and even Jesus himself suffer from baldness. All this loss of hair—and the grotesque pantomime that accompanies it—can be attributed to anxiety, guilt, shame, madness. Susan E. Meigs, however, conjectures that the men's bald heads "indicate the martyrdom of Christ and Lumumba."[6] More likely, though, is Werner Sollors's interpretation that "as the hair comes to an independent, horrifying life of its own, the living beings from whose head it comes are closer to death."[7]

Sarah's paranoia is thus colored by the distorted signifiers of her ancestry. Wanting to change her racial identity, she is obsessed with becoming white. "Whiteness is ingrained in her roots."[8] The title of Frantz Fanon's major work on race—*Black Skin, White Masks*[9]—precisely sums up Sarah's racial and psychic predicament. A revolutionary black writer whom Kennedy's husband knew and respected, Fanon is kidnapped in, and lines from his poetry are woven into, Kennedy's later plays, *The Film Club* and *Dramatic Circle*. Sarah, although she sees herself as "haunted" in her conception, yearns to cover her own black skin with a white mask and pass into white beauty, acceptance, and responsibility. (Appropriately, an ominous picture of Snow White is included in *People*.) Sarah's boyfriend Raymond is a young, white, Jewish poet; she herself lives in an apartment building with a white landlady, Mrs. Conrad. And Sarah obsesses in color-coded language and thinking. She puts "old photographs of castles and monarchs of England on her walls and venerated a gigantic plaster of Queen Victoria . . . a thing of astonishing whiteness" (14). In Kennedy's incantatory prose, Sarah confesses she is

preoccupied with the placement and geometric words on paper. I write poetry filling white page after white page with imitations of Edith Sitwell. It is my dream to live in rooms with European antiques and my Queen Victoria, photographs of Roman ruins, walls of books, a white glass table . . . My friends will be white. (14)

In her litany in admiration of whiteness, Sarah reveals that "I long to become even a more pallid Negro than I am now; pallid like Negroes on the covers of American Negro magazines;

soulless, educated and irreligious" (14). She is fixated on escaping a world where "black was evil," and, by extension, so is she. All of the artifacts that signify for Sarah a venerable and honorable white culture become "an embankment to keep me from reflecting too much upon the fact that I am a Negro" (14).

But as Kennedy's chilling play unravels, putting us in the middle of Sarah's nightmare, the tragic heroine cannot stop hallucinating about her tainted black ancestry and the (im)possibility of becoming white. Yet it is only a fantasy that she acquires a white identity. She foolishly tries to rationalize that "like all educated Negroes—out of life and death essential—I find it necessary to maintain a stark fortress against recognition of myself" (14). But her dreams offer no fortress; she cannot escape herself. Terrifyingly, she learns that the more she tries to flee her dark side, the more it follows her in the nightmare of her existence, as if in her own film noir. The white world offers neither refuge nor hope, no matter how lyrically powerful her fantasies. As *Funnyhouse of a Negro* irrevocably demonstrates, Sarah is victimized racially, sexually, and psychically. Helene Keyssar aptly describes Sarah's tragedy: "*Funnyhouse* is not an examination of a woman's idiosyncratic dissolution into madness but is an enacted metaphor—a genuine dramatization—of cultural structures that make self-deceit and mendacity viable alternatives to self-hatred for a person who is black and female."[10]

Setting—literal, symbolic, and psychic—is central to Kennedy's purpose in *Funnyhouse of a Negro*. In her first mad aria or monologue, Sarah reveals, "I live in my room. It is a small room on the top floor of a brownstone in the West Nineties in New York, a room filled with my dark old volumes, a narrow bed, and on the wall old photographs of castles and monarchs of England" (13). Like Albee's *The Zoo Story, Funnyhouse of a*

Negro takes place in the scarred cityscape of New York.[11] In fact, Jerry in *The Zoo Story* and Sarah live in the same blighted neighborhood of the West Nineties and confront many of the same absurdities of relationships, linking *Funnyhouse of a Negro* and *The Zoo Story* on one level as plays of urban alienation. But in terms of Kennedy's color symbolism, it seems ironically appropriate for the Negro Sarah to live in a "brownstone." Even so, the *Funnyhouse of a Negro* setting—like its characters—should not be read realistically. Sarah is the madwoman in a fictionalized brownstone; her room is quintessential psychic space. Emphasizing the fluidity of that psychic space, Kennedy's opening stage direction points out:

> *Funnyhouse of a Negro* is perhaps clearest and most explicit when the play is placed in the girl Sarah's room. The center of the stage works well as her room, allowing the rest of the stage as the place for herselves. . . . When she is placed in her room with her belongings, then the director is free to let the rest of the play happen around her. (11)

Sarah's room is transformed into the stage for her schizophrenic play. It is an infernal torture chamber, a prison of her mind with ghosts, dark hallways, and a plethora of grotesque visual and aural horrors. Self-deceivingly referring to her room as a "stark fortress" (14), Sarah pretends it will protect her, but it is transformed into the scene of a hellish nightmare where she commits suicide. The stage for this nightmare juxtaposes wildly dissimilar spaces, including a royal drawing room in London and an African jungle replete with "black grass."

Sarah's belongings become key props in this drama of her divided self. They are the possessions of the dispossessed, not the icons of acceptance by a white society, that speak about a devastating psychic past and underscore Sarah's futile attempts to find love and approval. On Sarah's walls, "old photographs of castles and monarchs of England" mock her (13). Seeking to become encrusted with a decaying, white past, Sarah dreams of living in "rooms with European antiques [and] photographs of Roman ruins" (19). But her pictures are hauntingly sterile. Instead of family albums, she displays photos of ruins, pointing toward the inevitable conclusion that her family—like her dreams to join the white world—has been leveled, broken, fragmented. She, too, is in ruins. Like Clara in *The Owl Answers,* Sarah is a black woman living in a white world and thus has "no ancestral roots."[12]

In a telling parallel, her black father's apartment in Harlem is also said to contain antique photos, undercutting Sarah's failure to escape her racial past and be seen as white. Her cherished "walls of books" (14), with their many "dark old volumes," symbolize her hope to escape the black world through education. Like later Kennedy heroines, Sarah is a sensitive young woman, an English major and a bibliophile; she works, reclusively, in a library. But again like the photos of ruins on her walls, her books remind Sarah of the futility of escaping her bleak environment through fiction. These books of damaging fiction about white heroines and heroes are filled with the white lies at the core of Sarah's psychodrama.

Undeniably, the most important object in Sarah's room is the grotesque "gigantic plaster statue of Queen Victoria" (13), a parody of the large statue of Victoria in front of Buckingham Palace that Kennedy saw on her trip to London in 1960.[13] Speaking reverently about this statue, Sarah observes that the "three steps that I contrived out of boards lead to the statue which I have placed opposite the door as I enter the room" (13). The plaster statue is an evocative religious and political symbol in Sarah's life. Paradoxically, she deifies it as a monument and refuge, but it also serves as a guard in her cruel prison of entrapment. As an idol, Victoria's statue distances Sarah from the black world she fears is going to engulf her. Yet this statue, like the character Queen Victoria herself, who represents one of Sarah's white selves, deceives and damns Sarah. It is a blasphemous icon of Sarah's false faith. There is no solace or validation for Sarah in owning this plaster statue, just another renunciation of self. The statue is "a thing of terror . . . suggesting large and probable deaths" (14), one of them being her own. Sarah worships the cold, false statue of the British queen to have a sense of owning part of a venerable white past, of belonging to a noble family.

Overall, though, Sarah's replica of the British queen is still another terrifying imitation. As Kennedy insists, "one must always fight against that imitation of one's self."[14] Yet Sarah does not fight against such imitations but instead allows them to proliferate in her life, just as Clara does in *A Movie Star Has to Star in Black and White* by allowing Hollywood film idols to "speak for her" and to "star in her life." Sarah even permits "imitation" to take over her writing by "filling white page after white page with imitations of Edith Sitwell" (14), the early modern English poet (1887–1964) known as "a shock-trooper of the poetic avant-garde" who, appropriately, wrote a biography entitled *Victoria of England*.[15] Like so many of Kennedy's heroines, Sarah's own voice and desires as a writer are thwarted in slavish imitation of a white author's works.

Under the spell of her hallucinations, Sarah transforms her room into a funnyhouse, the shaping motif and perhaps most important symbol in Kennedy's canon. In fact, the funnyhouse is the magnet toward which all of Sarah's nightmares are drawn and against which they are framed. This symbol has been variously interpreted as "an amusement park of the imagination," a "funnyhouse of feelings," and a "crazyhouse for minorities" destroyed by delusions.[16] It is the funnyhouse of Sarah's madness. Kennedy came upon the idea for a funnyhouse from a Cleveland amusement park that featured one as a main attraction, with two grotesquely laughing white clown figures guarding either side of its entrance. She replicates these clowns in *Funnyhouse of a Negro* through Raymond, the Funnyhouse Man, and Mrs. Conrad, the Funnyhouse Lady, who mock Sarah with their cruel laughter. "The poor bitch has hung herself," sneers Mrs. Conrad, while Raymond rejoins, "She was a funny little liar" (25). In a 1984 production of *Funnyhouse of a Negro* at New York University, the white actors playing Raymond and Mrs. Conrad sported large red circles painted on their pasty cheeks in order to parody circus clowns, an appropriate costume for the sinister, carnivalesque atmosphere of Kennedy's play. The funnyhouse, then, becomes the perfect surrealistic setting for Sarah's dreams to be projected on stage. It pulls so much together in Kennedy's play, in a manner similar to the dream sequences in August Strindberg's expressionistic plays or the mounds of earth in Samuel Beckett's *Happy Days*. Beyond doubt, too, the funnyhouse imparts a harrowing "Kafkaesque quality" to Kennedy's work.[17]

A funnyhouse is made up of rows or walls of mirrors that distort the images they reflect, making some parts bigger while shrinking others, especially heads, or even making some parts vanish altogether. In "Because of the King of France," Sidney's dreams of being a white artist accepted by Louis XIV are symbolically shattered in "the Hall of Mirrors" (6). Funnyhouse Man Raymond is aptly associated with mirrors behind blinds that he "*keeps opening and closing*" to reveal a "partially disrobed Duchess" (16), as if he were offering a freakish peep show. Throughout, he "*walks about the place opening the blinds and laughing.*" In a production of *Funnyhouse of a Negro* in San Francisco at the Intersection for the Arts in May 2000, Sarah was "surrounded with fun-house mirrors glinting behind strips of gauzy white film, so that everywhere she sees a warped projection of herself, looming and scared."[18] In such a setting, the self is visually torn apart, parceled into fragments. In a funnyhouse, one's identity and self-image are never stable, reliable, truthful, or comforting. Representation in Kennedy's funnyhouse leads to self-repression and revulsion. Tormented by racist views of herself, Sarah cannot avoid the delusions of her funnyhouse breakdown when she looks at herself or at others. In this funnyhouse of her mind, Sarah's fear and guilt become magnified, distorted, dismembered. She has no perspective. Time, place, and hope dissolve. The shocking world of the funnyhouse also symbolizes her mad fantasies and the impossibility of escape. As psychotherapist Gaetano Benedetti contends, "Hallucinations of mad people are dreams from which they cannot awake."[19]

Through staging, props, and characterization, Kennedy's play incorporates many of the phantasmagoric effects of living in a funnyhouse. Physical boundaries disappear as characters come through the walls of the set (15), or walls simply drop down out of sight (19). Lighting is dark and shadowy, and then, without warning, blackouts shroud audiences in dread, rendering them fearful of what's happening and what's coming next, again reminiscent of film noir. According to Erin Hurley, the blackouts "punctuate the narrative and indicate a change in location or time. They also frustrate attempts at making clear and 'logical' sense of the plot or characters; each time one approaches insight, Kennedy cuts the power."[20] Locations change, blur, loom threateningly ahead, or are distorted as if "almost standing still in a dream." One minute we are in a queen's drawing room, and in the next Sarah sees her father coming through a jungle to menace her. Kennedy floods the stage with tawdry spectacle. In part of Sarah's room we see "*a chandeliered ballroom with* SNOW *falling . . . a bench decorated with white flowers . . . made of obviously fake materials as they would be in a funnyhouse*" (21). As in a "spook house," strange, vile creatures pop out of nowhere. A "*red sun*" and "*flying things*" (23) whiz by Sarah, as do ominous "*great black ravens*" (12). Kennedy's terrifying birds have been traced to Edgar Allan Poe's death-shaded poem "The Raven."[21]

A cacophony of sounds accompanies these grotesque sights. Screams, cries, and jeering laughter destroy Sarah's mind and the audience's peace. The cruel laughter of Kennedy's funnyhouse occurs at strategic points, most notably, for example, when a "*bald head is dropped on a string*" (21) or when Sarah is ridiculed by Raymond and Mrs. Conrad. Tormenting laughter often accompanies the frightening heads severed from bodies in *Funnyhouse of a Negro*. Dismembered, disembodied heads visually represent a mind gone mad, torn from the body of reason in the ghastly corridors of Sarah's nightmare. As we saw, Sarah's mad mother carries a bald head before her. Another crucial sound is Sarah's father's incessant knocking, also linking Kennedy's play to "The Raven," where we hear someone "gently rapping, knocking at my chamber door." An equally convincing case might be made that the sound of Sarah's father's knocking may echo the death-knell knocking of the porter of "Hell Gate" in *Macbeth* (2.3), announcing the intrusion of the infernal into the world of the living. Moreover, Sarah's mother, dressed in her nightgown and beset by nightmares, approximates a guilt-ridden Lady Macbeth.

But most important, the funnyhouse motif, with its distortions and disorientation, facilitates the key structural element in Kennedy's play—Sarah's projections of, or pluralizations into, her various selves. In her stream of (un)consciousness, she creates four different personalities, or figures, to speak for her, to tell her story, to repeat her lines, often verbatim—Queen Victoria, the Duchess of Hapsburg, Patrice Lumumba, and Jesus Christ. Susan Sontag characterized *Funnyhouse of a Negro* as a play about "a deranged girl in colloquy with four incarnate ideas of her self."[22] As Lois More Overbeck points out, "In a sense, [Sarah] stops speaking after the first third of the play, but she is still there, and she 'speaks' through the other voices."[23] These characters are Sarah's "schizophrenic voices" through which her trauma is "recycled and mirrored."[24] They are the alters in her dissociative world, or what Werner Sollors calls "a collage of multifaceted, contradictory selves,"[25] the composite picture of her tormented psychic being.

These four selves represent Sarah's psychic family and her racial and sexual past, reflecting the sensibilities and tastes of this young black woman who loves to study European poetry and culture, work in libraries, and hang pictures of castles and ruins on her walls. In describing the room of her mind, Sarah makes spatial and relationship places for these four selves. Confessing that they are her selves, she maps out the psychic dramaturgy of her stage: "When I am the Duchess of Hapsburg I sit opposite Victoria in my headpiece and we talk" (14). "Part of the time I live with Raymond," and "part of the time with God, Maxmilian and Albert Saxe Coburg" (14), Victoria's husband whom she mourned for over forty years. Accompanied by her selves, Sarah journeys into her interior world of secrets, fears, and confusions.

In creating four highly symbolic selves for Sarah, Kennedy abandons the singular "I," signifying one person, for the psychotic "We" or "All," as a speech prefix labels these four characters when they talk in unison at the end of *Funnyhouse of a Negro*. In so doing, Kennedy challenges the very idea of a dramatic character who displays a clear-cut, focused identity. Using these four selves, Kennedy takes audiences into a new world of postidentity, crossing and collapsing racial, gender, ethnic, political, and historical boundaries. Jesus and Lumumba represent Sarah's male side, while Victoria and the Duchess stand for the female side. The two women act like white aristocrats (though the Duchess calls herself "yellow," [12]), while Lumumba—called simply Man in the play—is black and Jesus is represented as a distorted, yellow dwarf. Each of these symbolic characters reflects Sarah's desire to be white as well as the impossibility of her attempt. Being black, white, and yellow, these four figures, all representing Sarah, visually emphasize that she does not fit securely into any one racial category, least of all that of a white person. In Sarah's quest for whiteness, then, these four selves actually undercut the facade of hope she erects to be seen as a white woman.

In costume and makeup, Sarah's four selves accentuate the distortions of her unrealistic, funnyhouse world. Hardly regal, the women wear "*cheap satin*," garish period costumes. The Duchess and Queen Victoria "*look exactly alike and will wear masks or be made up to appear a whitish yellow. It is an alabaster face, the skin drawn tightly over the cheekbones, great dark eyes that seem gouged out of the head, a high forehead, a full red mouth and a head of frizzy hair. If the characters do not wear a mask, then the face must be highly powdered . . . a quality and a stillness as in the face of death"* (12). Their makeup and appearance are grotesque, suggesting the funnyhouse world of disturbing harlequins. According to Billie Allen, who played Sarah in the 1964 premiere, "They are black people who want to be white."[26] But Kennedy goes further than just commenting on a black person passing for white. By shockingly showing us an actor underneath the character, she reveals how dangerously deceptive and artificial role-playing can be. These distorted portrayals of the Duchess and Victoria are the way Sarah, the mulatta who wants to be white, envisions herself, with her kinky hair and guilt-ridden soul. Under the representation are her self-loathing and self-denial. The representations of Lumumba and Jesus also reflect the funnyhouse of her mind, with its illusions and hallucinations. The men's costumes and appearances are suitably and terrifyingly freakish, distorted. *"Jesus is a hunchback, yellow-skinned dwarf, dressed in white rags and sandals."* Patrice Lumumba is a black man whose *"head appears to be split in two with blood and tissue in eyes. He carries an ebony mask"* (15). Kennedy revolutionizes the conventions of realistic/naturalistic theater to project even more violently Sarah's racial, sexual, and political nightmare through her male selves.

Of these four selves, though, Queen Victoria is unarguably at the center of Sarah's hallucinations of wanting to be white. She is "my idol," confesses Sarah. In *People,* Kennedy expressed her amazement that any one person, such as Victoria, could have an era or age named after herself or himself. Through her

Victoria self, Sarah hopes to lay claim to the respectability, pol-
ish, and power of that era by emulating and assimilating the values of high Victorian culture, with its implacable moral and
sexual codes.[27] For more than sixty years, Victoria Regina
(1837–1901) reigned over a British empire that ruled much of
the world—from the British Raj in India to parliamentary procedures in Africa, New Guinea, and the Far East. Victorian
colonists traveled into the jungles to subjugate nonwhites and
convert them to a color-based Christianity.

As Sarah, Victoria anachronistically laments that her black
father "is arriving again for the night. He comes through the
jungle to find me. He never tires of his journey" (12). Victoria's
chamber and Lumumba's (the father's) jungle become key
metaphoric spaces in Sarah's twisted psychic journey through
history. Africans, like Sarah's father, did not leave the jungle to
search for white mothers or daughters, as *Funnyhouse of a
Negro* tragically insists. Reversing the direction of colonial dom-
inance to accommodate her own psychic history, Sarah as Victoria is "still a victim of colonization."[28] Victoria's appearance
proves that Sarah cannot escape her blackness no matter how
historically lofty her hallucinations are. As one of Sarah's selves,
Victoria has kinky hair and a "cheap white satin" dress that are
at odds with the appearance of the actual queen. The black
actress with frizzy hair playing the queen in Sarah's nightmare
jarringly contrasts with the "astonishing whiteness" of Victoria's statue in Sarah's room.

The Duchess of Hapsburg is another female ruler whom
Sarah imagines herself to be. As the wife of Maximilian Hapsburg, heir to the Austro-Hungarian Empire, the Duchess Carlota went to Mexico in the 1860s to colonize her darker subjects
and thus begin an empire propped up by the unscrupulous Louis

Napoleon III. When Maximilian's rule was overthrown and he was executed, Carlota went mad, suggesting further links between this self of Sarah's and her own mad mother. The Hapsburgs's tragic fate was the subject of a 1939 film, *Juarez,* starring Kennedy's favorite movie star, Bette Davis, as Carlota. In 1957, Kennedy visited the Chapultepec Palace, from where the Hapsburgs ruled, and recorded: "I bought many post cards of the palace and the Duchess of Hapsburg and saved them. One day the Duchess of Hapsburg would become one of my characters' most sympathetic alter egos or selves" (*People,* 96). Like Victoria, the Duchess mocks Sarah's dream of escaping into white power. She turns out to be black underneath, with a black face and frizzy hair beneath her white mask or makeup. Again, a passage from *People* about the Hapsburgs's colonization in Mexico is relevant to Sarah's fate. "There seemed something amiss," concluded Kennedy, about "European royalty in an alien landscape." Kennedy has brilliantly mapped the anxiety and dissonance of that landscape in *Funnyhouse of a Negro* by having the Duchess "exist in an alien persona, that of the Negro writer" (97).

Yet even more than Queen Victoria, the Duchess expresses Sarah's dread over her approaching black father. Given more lines than Victoria, the Duchess bristles, "How dare he enter the castle" (12), and later pleads, "Hide me." Like Sarah's mother, the Duchess fears being raped by a black man, precisely Sarah's fears as well. As Sarah's Duchess self exclaims, "My father is a nigger who drives me to misery. Any time spent with him evolves itself into suffering. He is a black man and the wilderness" (17). Like a funnyhouse theater manager, the Duchess invites others to watch and participate in her spectacle. In another harrowing example of Kennedy's stage poetry, she tells

Jesus "I have something to show you," and then *"slowly removes her headpiece and from under it takes a mass of her hair"* (21). Uncovering layers of consciousness and artifice, Kennedy discloses an actress playing a mad woman (Sarah) playing a mad duchess (Carlota), blurring and merging historical event and personal history.

Kennedy's theater of selves is as complex politically as it is psychologically. Historically, white rulers such as Victoria and Carlota constructed identity based on culture, class, and race. According to their colonial imperatives, people were placed into opposing, dichotomous categories—white/black, colonists/colonized, majority/Other, civilized/savage. Such a binary system favored the dominant white society, which always pictured itself as better, brighter, more fit to rule. Such a classification typifies the clash between white Europeans and black Africans at the core of so many Kennedy plays.[29] In selecting Victoria and Carlota as two of Sarah's selves, and depicting Sarah's Otherness by projecting it through them, Kennedy politically stresses how categories of opposites were used to justify the oppression and the exclusion of Sarah as a black woman. Sadly, even within her selves, Sarah is stigmatized as inferior, an outcast.

Still other political implications surface in having Sarah's Duchess and Victoria dress in white faces. Studying *Funnyhouse of a Negro* as a parody of minstrelsy, where black actors wearing white faces imitated a colonizing white audience on nineteenth- and early twentieth-century stages, Jacqueline Wood perceptively argues that "Queen Victoria and the Duchess emerge as loci of power informed by contemporary global experiences of patriarchal imperialism and racism. They are dominant white figures, superimposed upon blackness, symbolizing the political imposition of European power over black—read

African society—here." Yet, as Wood concludes, "the black Sarah underneath that whiteness ironically reveals how these two royal selves violently obtrude upon Sarah's blackness, how they impose a destructive self-hatred, raising the stakes of ever attaining any personal resolution."[30] Studying the practice of white actors wearing blackface in twentieth-century drama, Susan Gubar similarly concludes that rather than subverting racial stereotypes, such costuming actually empowers the white body underneath the blackface.[31]

Patrice Lumumba, another one of Sarah's selves or alters, also represents a political and racial Other. The real-life Lumumba was the first premier of Zaire (now the Democratic Republic of Congo), assassinated only a few years after the once colonial country gained its independence. In fact, Lumumba died while Kennedy was in Ghana in 1961, a full three years before *Funnyhouse of a Negro* premiered Off Broadway. Jochen Achilles calls him the "representative of a rebellious and self-confident African city," and Margaret Wilkerson honors him as a "martyred leader, representing emerging African nations."[32] Unquestionably, Lumumba is the most horrifying, gory character in *Funnyhouse of a Negro*. "*His head appears to be split in two with blood and tissue in his eyes. He carries an ebony mask*" (15), a prop both vital to the African rituals and drama Kennedy witnessed in Ghana and as an icon of identity. In his function as one of Sarah's selves, Lumumba symbolizes her martyrdom, too, by white enemies, and thus prefigures her gruesome death by hanging at the end of the play. His split head visually represents the psychic/racial strife that tears Sarah apart and shows that black women are not the only victims of violence in Kennedy's canon.

But Lumumba occupies one of the most paradoxical roles in Sarah's nightmare world. Like her other selves, he does not play a static, univocal role, but is part of a transformative drama. More than just playing the role of a martyr, Lumumba becomes one of Sarah's most harrowing, combative alters, intensifying the tragic consequences of her fictions, her hallucinations. For instance, he significantly changes lines that Sarah and the Duchess have previously spoken. "It is also my nigger dream for my friends to eat their meals on white glass tables and to live in rooms with European antiques, photographs of Roman nuns. . . . My friends will be white. I need them as an embankment to keep me from reflecting too much upon the fact that I am Patrice Lumumba who haunted my mother's conception" (19). By labeling himself a "nigger" and indicting himself (as a representation of Sarah's black father) as the one who haunted his mother's conception, Lumumba irrevocably compels Sarah to admit her African roots and to forget any pretenses or pretext of being white royalty. Like Sarah's father's, Lumumba's blackness cannot be doubted—racially, politically, sexually. He is the most fearsome of Sarah's selves.

To deepen the tragic horror even more, Kennedy orchestrates a series of structural parallels between Lumumba and Sarah's father. Lumumba casts himself in Sarah's father's shadow with his monologue that begins: "I am a nigger of two generations. I am Patrice Lumumba. I am a nigger of two generations. I am the black shadow that haunted my mother's conception. I belong to the generation born at the turn of the century . . . At present I reside in New York City in a brownstone in the West Nineties" (19). Kennedy provocatively fuses a black male self with a light-skinned female self—in syntax, word choice, rhythm—to stage the warring generational and racial voices inside Sarah's psyche. As Robert Scanlon points out, "Kennedy certainly was not jumping on any contemporary bandwagons when she painted such a dreadful portrait of this black progenitor. 'I am a nigger of two generations' says this faceless figure, meaning he infected the mother with blackness and engendered a second degree of blackness in her daughter, [the] protagonist Sarah."[33] In this context, Lumumba (or more likely his ghost) came out of the jungle and merged in Sarah's imagination with her rapist father. The way Sarah is said to have murdered her father is the way in which Lumumba met his death.[34] She bludgeons him with the African mask, cracking his skull like Lumumba's. Visually, Lumumba's mask is analogous to the one that Sarah's father carries. All of Sarah's selves cry out against the dreaded, masked father at the end of *Funnyhouse of a Negro:* "I see him. The black ugly thing is sitting in his hallway, surrounded by his ebony masks" (24).

Although Lumumba might be the play's most gory character, the figure of Jesus as one of Sarah's selves is beyond doubt the most distorted portrait in *Funnyhouse of a Negro.* Sarah's Jesus is not the loving, forgiving Christ of the New Testament or the suffering Savior of Mel Gibson's film *The Passion of the Christ,* but a lascivious and vile dwarf who courts the Duchess (21–22). The 1995 Signature Theatre production presented "an autistic Jesus . . . who suggest[ed] a black flower child of the late 1960s."[35] Rejected by the bigoted religion of a white establishment, like Brother and Sister Rat in *A Rat's Mass,* Sarah creates a terrifying yellow Jesus out of her fear and frenzy. The distorted, dwarfed Jesus is her image of a corrupt theology of colonialism that infantalized, colonized, and racialized subjects, turning them into unfit heirs to the Kingdom of Heaven. As a vengeful Sarah who is denied salvation because she is black, Jesus seethes: "I am going to Africa and kill this black man named Patrice Lumumba. Why? Because all my life I believed my Holy Father to be God, but now I know my father is a black man" (23). In Sarah's nightmare, the figure of Jesus is thus heinously incorporated into the character of Man/Lumumba/father, whose mother wanted him to be a "savior of the race" and hoped "he would be Christ but he failed" (22).

Sarah's Jesus is another representative of her despair, the reason she wears a rope around her neck. In soul, as in body, Sarah cannot escape being black. Ironically, she dreams of salvation and heaven through lyrical, African allusions: "I wanted to live in Genesis in the midst of golden savannahs" (21). Sollors glosses "Genesis" as Lake Gennesaret in St. Mark.[36] But, more likely, Kennedy intended Genesis to stand for a prelapsarian Eden that a sanctified (golden = white) Sarah hoped for. But, like her father, she must say, "I wanted to be a Christian. Now I am Judas" (21). In this climactic moment of Sarah's hallucinatory drama, she turns her hope of salvation in Jesus into her betrayal as and through a black man.

Although not widely staged, *Funnyhouse of a Negro* has received important productions as directors (re)interpret Kennedy's script. On 8 March 1969, *Drôle de baraque,* a French translation of *Funnyhouse of a Negro* directed by Jean-Marie Serreau, premiered at Le Petit Odeon in Paris, and was compared to Eugene O'Neill's *Emperor Jones* in part because of its "dance macabre rhythms."[37] On 28 April 1968, a British *Funnyhouse of a Negro,* directed by Rob Knights and starring Sheila Wilkinson, opened at the Royal Court Theatre in London. This production used a color-coded set of "old yellowed walls," appropriate for Sarah's skin color and the withered antiquity she enshrines, and for the "final image" audiences saw "a corpse hurtling from the flies, the white skull severed from its black body."[38] The critics read *Funnyhouse of a Negro* primarily as a "racial allegory."[39] Preceding the performance, audiences were given "musical entertainment" from Ginger Johnson and his African Drummers, one of whom put on a display of fire-eating, ironically the kind of racialized performance Sarah wanted to flee. In the 1995 Signature Theatre's production, director Caroline Jackson Smith believed that even though Sarah was "the central figure . . . she [was] more the lead instrument in a piece of chamber music than the leading lady in a conventional drama."[40] Sarah's warring selves, however, turned chamber music into mad cries.

CHAPTER 3

Cities in Bezique

The Owl Answers and A Beast Story

Cities in Bezique, published in 1969, contains two plays—*The Owl Answers* and *A Beast Story.*[1] Kennedy regards *The Owl Answers* as her "favorite play";[2] it may also be her most complex work. Written when *Funnyhouse of a Negro* was in workshop, *The Owl Answers* premiered in 1965 at the White Barn Theatre in Connecticut and then at New York's Theatre de Lys, where it was directed by Michael Kahn. In 1969, it ran for three months, along with *A Beast Story,* at the New York Shakespeare Festival Public Theater, where it was directed by Gerald Freedman. Joe Papp, one of Kennedy's mentors and the Festival founder, claimed it was her best-written play.[3] A significant revival of *The Owl Answers* came to Chicago's Goodman Theatre in 1997.

A Beast Story (written in 1961), on the other hand, may be Kennedy's least-studied and least-performed play. She claims it is her least favorite. After its publication in *Cities in Bezique,* it was reprinted only once in the collection *Kuntu Drama: Plays of the African Continuum.*[4] Kennedy did not want it anthologized in either *Adrienne Kennedy in One Act* or *The Adrienne Kennedy Reader.* Studying it in conjunction with *The Owl Answers,* Kimberly W. Benston sees *A Beast Story* as a "diptych," "essentially an extension of *Owl* in theme and technique."[5] *The Owl Answers* and *A Beast Story* also share character types, imagery, and dramaturgy with *Funnyhouse of a Negro, A Rat's Mass,* and *Sun.*

The collective title under which these plays have been staged—*Cities in Bezique*—has puzzled readers. But Kennedy's title does link the two and helps explain them thematically and structurally. Bezique is a card game that originated in France but was also very popular in Britain. "There are at least six forms of the game and these variations depend on the number of players participating."[6] Like this card game, Kennedy's characters go through a series of transformations, or variations. Their identities are declared, reshuffled, recombined, and shifted from one player to another, all within the plays' urban settings (or the characters' psychological spaces). Ironically, though, there are no winners in Kennedy's cities of the mind; each player or identity is ultimately exchanged, trumped, and penalized until she or he is discarded.

The Owl Answers

Kennedy continues her dramatization of a black woman's search for identity in a hostile white world in *The Owl Answers*. Clara Passmore in *The Owl Answers* is a soul sister of Sarah in *Funnyhouse of a Negro;* their names even rhyme. Both are highly literate, light-skinned ("pallid") black women betrayed by family and by an Anglo-Saxon society whose approval they desperately seek but from whose bastions of power they are excluded. Aspiring writers, they are both "afflicted with Gertrude Stein nervousness."[7] Clara, who is called She, is submerged in a surrealistic nightmare encompassing many of the fears that rip Sarah apart. Both characters' psychic journeys take them into a fantastic world where time and place are distorted and where historical characters mix with individuals from these heroines' personal histories to indict and to terrorize them. In expressing their collective and personal guilt, Clara and Sarah undergo the struggle of "the Afro-American's soul life."[8] Confronting self and the condemnation of white society and its punitive Christianity, these women are condemned to live in two worlds—white and black—simultaneously. Ultimately, Clara, like Sarah, is destroyed for daring to cross the color line.

Although they share common characteristics, Clara and Sarah display their fragmented identities in different ways. In *Funnyhouse of a Negro,* Sarah projects her various selves or states of mind through a host of separate characters—Queen Elizabeth, Lumumba, and so forth—outside herself. Yet in *The Owl Answers,* She/Clara contains within herself a "composite of multiple identities," or "irreconcilable selves,"[9] something like three Joanne Woodwards simultaneously performing *Three Faces of Eve.* Multiple identities, all of them She/Clara, all the time, reside in "She who is Clara Passmore who is the Virgin Mary who is the Bastard who is the Owl." These various identities and roles are entangled in a cluster of relationships, too: "Clara, the Negro child of Rev. Passmore; Mary, the martyred Virgin; Bastard, the mulatto daughter of the Dead White Father . . . and at last . . . the mysterious Owl."[10]

In projecting these alternating and conflicting identities, *The Owl Answers* demonstrates an even more violent distortion of self than *Funnyhouse of a Negro* does. Perhaps no other play better illustrates Kennedy's fascination with transformations of self than does *The Owl Answers.* Susan Booth, who directed the Goodman Theatre revival in 1997, summarized how She feels: "You walk down the street and you are white girl you are black guy you are rich you are lucky you are ugly you are in you are out you are whatever the seer sees and transcribes you to be [*sic*]."[11] Other characters blend into several selves, too, reflecting She's different identities. "The Black Bastard Mother who is the Reverend's Wife who is Anne Boleyn," and the Father is "the Richest White Man in the Town who is the Dead White Father who is Reverend Passmore" (29). As Walter Kerr concludes, "Everyone is possibly everyone else and the girl is possibly all of them."[12]

Kennedy's opening stage direction explains the dramaturgy of these in-dwelling multiple personalities. "The characters change slowly back and forth into and out of themselves, leaving some garment from their previous selves upon them always to remind us of the nature of She who is Clara Passmore who is the Virgin Mary who is the Bastard who is the Owl's world" (29). A symbol of identity as well as an index to occupation and personality, the "garment of clothing" seemingly promises continuity from one character to another but actually disrupts an audience's attempt to separate or coordinate She and her separate identities. With just a single change of costume, one character immediately turns into another. Reviewing the 1969 Public Theater production, Richard P. Cooke pointed out, "One character may be represented by more than one actor or actress, with imaginary flashes in kaleidoscope fashion."[13] In addition to costume changes, black actors wear white masks, as in *Funnyhouse of a Negro,* to portray white characters, further complicating the issue of identity.

She's fractured selves (and those of other characters in her family) are intentionally dislocated and disarming. By splitting a character into her individual and collective identities, Kennedy emphasizes She's alienation from herself and from others. She is white and She is black; She is the Virgin Mary and a Harlem whore; She is literate and yet is reduced to a moaning owl. She lives in the present and the past at the same time. In essence, She is a fragmented soul who does not fit in. She lives in a world splintered by the same contradictions embodied in Clara Passmore. This is She/Clara's tragic ancestry and her legacy, which marks the other "children of mixed birth" (*Deadly Triplets*, 19) that cry throughout Kennedy's works.

Like other Kennedy plays, *The Owl Answers* has its roots in her family history. She/Clara is an amalgam of Kennedy's Aunt Martha, her own mother, and herself. Speaking of her aunt, Kennedy recalled:

> Clara's was very much like my aunt's life. She was this girl who grew up in a small Georgia town. She was quite brilliant. Her father was white. She came to live with us when I was in high school. They wanted her to go to school in Cleveland because they figured she was so smart . . . she got her Masters at Teacher's College at Columbia. She teaches English somewhere in the South now. I used to listen to her talk a lot. She was very hysterical . . . what struck me as a young person was how she used to talk, how she didn't belong anywhere. She's very much the basis for that girl in *The Owl Answers*.[14]

In *People*, we learn that Aunt Martha, "pretty with freckles and brown curly hair," influenced her niece Adrienne's reading and, eventually, her character Clara. Like Clara, Martha savored Shakespeare, whom she shared with the young Kennedy: "She read to me from *Romeo and Juliet* . . . and told me she was also reading Shakespeare's sonnets." Kennedy continues, "When I thought no one was looking, I tried to read her books, and sometimes, if I was quiet enough, she would let me study with her" (102). Kennedy's mother, Aunt Martha's half sister, also reminded her of Clara in terms of her love of learning and her unconventional pursuit of a life of the mind in Cleveland in the 1930s. "I think my mother marked me."[15]

Most important, however, *The Owl Answers* grew out of Kennedy's own experiences in Ghana in the 1960s. In *People,* she recorded that

> the owls in the trees outside the Achimota Guest House were close, and at night, because we slept under gigantic mosquito nets, I felt enclosed in their sound. In the mornings I would try to find the owls in the trees but could never see them. Yet, at night in the shuttered room, under the huge white canopied nets, the owls sounded as if they were in the very center of the room.
>
> I was pregnant again. And there were difficulties. I had to stay in bed for a week, as I bled. I listened to the owl sounds, afraid. In a few months I would create a character who would turn into an owl. (121–22)

That character, of course, is Clara Passmore, She, whose psychic history is told in and through the mysterious language of owl-dom. The owl, as we shall see, becomes the dark voice of the night haunting Clara as it did the pregnant Kennedy, who could not find the owls in the daylight world where reason, not haunted nightmares, supposedly dominates.

Like *Funnyhouse of a Negro, The Owl Answers* is staged in four highly symbolic and expressionistic settings or spaces reflecting the heroine's living, subconsciously, in many worlds. In contrast to Sarah's crowded room in *Funnyhouse of a Negro,* the scene in *The Owl Answers* "*is a New York subway is the Tower of London is a Harlem hotel room is St. Peter's*" (29).

While each of these four locations is vastly different, geographically and culturally, they merge in She's mind to express the racial, religious, and political conflicts in her subconscious. Clive Barnes commented that as the play opens, we see "a light-skinned yet black girl . . . sitting in a subway train minding her own dreams."[16] Even so, most of the action in *The Owl Answers* emanates from, through, or around the subway as characters enter or exit through its gates and doors. As the subway doors open, we see "*The gates, the High Altar, the ceiling and the Dome are like St. Peter's*" (30), which lie just beyond the subway set. These gates represent many places on stage while "*the walls of the subway set are like the Tower of London.*" The High Altar and Dome of St. Peter's signal a shift to events involving the Reverend Passmore and the Black Mother, or taking place in She's Harlem hotel room. References to the tower gates mark Clara's imprisonment in the London of her imagination. Kennedy develops these multiple sets the same way she does her characters, by projecting them through their multiple selves. Spaces, like characters, in Kennedy's theater are volatile.

The opening set of *The Owl Answers,* shaped like a New York subway car, uses the props—e.g., hand straps, doors—and subway sounds to assault an audience's psyche: "*The space should lurch, lights flash, gates slam*" (30). These are powerful expressionistic techniques that take us into the unknown terrors of She's frenzied black psyche. "The constant clang of the subway doors and the jolting stops and starts convey the sense that all the characters are on a ride they cannot control."[17] Like the subway, the characters are in a constant state of agitation and clanging flux. Signaling the whirling images in She's subconscious, the stage rotates—spins—as people get on and off the subway (33). This dark tunnel and the subway car are the perfect stages on which to perform She/Clara's nightmares, the aperture for her underground experiences. Unlike the naturalistic subways of Baraka's *Dutchman* or in the film *The Incident* (1967), Kennedy's framing set physicalizes the starts and stops—lunging and jolting—that She frenetically makes in her subconscious. In the caverns of this subway, She discloses her tormenting thoughts, dreams, and fears, thereby taking herself and the audience on a symbolic journey of self-discovery through the subway noises and lights that race by her. Traveling in a psychic whirlwind, She darts from one cultural space or site —the Tower of London, Harlem, St. Peter's—to another as her different states of mind or personalities flee from reality, imprisonment, and death. Through the subway set, then, Kennedy connects these disparate locations and stops in She's mind simultaneously, since all four sets are visible on stage.

But She/Clara's selves, like the events in her life, are not so easy to follow. Like *Funnyhouse of a Negro, The Owl Answers* is built on the fantastic, the obscure, the hysteric. There is no clear or sequential storyline or plot with differentiated and consistent places, events, characters, motives, and time frames. Characters have no stable identity; they have multiple personalities and identities that reconfigure without notice, precipitously. That the heroine is often referred to, both in speech prefixes and in dialogue, as the generic *She* illustrates how society has stripped Clara Passmore of a legal, stable, and comforting identity altogether. She is a victim of identity theft in a white racist society. Jeanie Forte summarizes the dilemma Kennedy's drama poses for an audience accustomed to a realistic, plot-driven theater.

The play's ambiguity and near incomprehensibility articulate the impossibility of identification with a narrative position, least of all one which might provide closure of the fiction of a coherent self. Clara—who is not one character, or person or subjectivity—instead traverses narrative, zig-zagging across various systems of signification, seeking herself in the gaps, the spaces of unnarrated silence wherein her persistently elusive subjectivity might be found.[18]

These impossibilities notwithstanding, Clara, like Sarah, does have a historical as well as psychic past helping audiences to interpret her chillingly tragic present. Of course, what precisely happened to She, when and where, is buried under the layers of her subconscious. Nevertheless, some crucial biographical details are recoverable within *The Owl Answers*'s fractured narrative.

She/Clara is both a child and victim of racial strife, mixed heritage, and psychic persecution. The Richest White Man in the Town, Mr. William Mattheson, and his black cook conceive a child; the cook is stigmatized as a whore and labeled the Bastard's Black Mother. The child of this union was adopted by a Southern black minister, Reverend Passmore, and his wife, who named her Clara but sometimes call her Mary. Enslaved to a decaying and colonizing Christianity, Reverend Passmore carries a "white battered Bible" (31), and "passes," as She tries to, in the white world. Like the sanctimonious and frightening preachers Kennedy remembered as a child, he condemns female sexuality, branding it carnal, sinful. Also obsessed with sexual purity, his wife sees their adopted daughter as sometimes virginal but more often as the Bastard, a sinner.

In She's nightmare world, her Black Mother commits suicide with a butcher knife on a bed transformed into a "burning altar" reminiscent of the baroque ornateness of St. Peter's Cathedral. "Taking a summer trip to London to see her white father's ancestors" (as Kennedy herself says of Clara in the preface to *Deadly Triplets* [ix]), She/Clara is forbidden to attend her white father's funeral but fantasizes about taking a trip to England with him where they visit the shrines of the pristine white culture She wants to claim as hers, too. But when her father dies, the literary figures She most admires—Chaucer and Shakespeare—prevent her from seeing him at St. Paul's Cathedral in London and, instead, lock her in the Tower of London. Whether earlier, later, or simultaneously (time does not follow sequentially in a Kennedy play), She leaves her job as a teacher in Savannah to seduce black men on the subway, taking them to her Harlem hotel room in search of love. When the Negro Man attempts to rape her, She fights him with a butcher knife, and is then transformed into an owl as her dead white father returns to blow out sacramental candles that burn in her hotel room.

In no other Kennedy play is a heroine more obsessed with finding her father and claiming his heritage as her own. She's identity is bound to her father's. Sarah, on the other hand, flees from her father, a Negro who haunts her. But She claims of the Richest White Man in the Town—"He is my father" (30)—and upon his death in England, she pleads, "I am almost white, am I not? Let me into St. Paul's Chapel. Let me please go down . . . I am his daughter" (31–32). But "almost" becomes the mantra of her legacy and her curse, thwarting her claims to be accepted by the white world. A delirious, self-encouraging Clara, white in her own mind, can proclaim, "I who am the ancestor of Shakespeare, Chaucer and William the Conqueror, I went to London" (36), but history stands against her. Her dead father bristles, "You are not my ancestor. You are my bastard. Keep her locked there, William" (33), speaking to William the Conqueror, the dynastic father of England after the Norman Conquest of 1076.

More logically put, She is her father's "descendant" rather than "ancestor." Yet, as Carla McDonough argues, "Clara's bastardy indicates that she bears the sins committed by her father and her mother because she herself is made to be also the cause of that sin—its originator or ancestor. By confusing 'ancestor' with 'descendant,' throughout . . . the dialogue plays upon the idea that history is always present: the past is never gone but endlessly repeated/re-enacted."[19] These cruel reversals and rejections counter She's fantasy acceptance by her white father and William the Conqueror. "We were wandering about the garden, you leaning on my arm, speaking of William the Conqueror" (33), She tells her fictionalized (benevolent) white father. But the idealized white father, Mr. William Mattheson, only joins King William to denounce her as a bastard, a black girl, unworthy even to make such genetic claims.

Kennedy's stagecraft graphically captures She/Clara's mixed, "almost" heritages by showing her two fathers, one white and one black, the former symbolically changing into the latter. "*The Dead Father appears dead. He is dead. Yet as She watches, he moves and comes to life. The Dead Father removes his hair, takes off his white face, from the chair he takes a white church robe and puts it on. Beneath his white hair is dark Negro hair. He is now Reverend Passmore*" (31). In the Public Theater production of 1969 these two fathers were played by the same actor, as was also done at the Goodman Theatre revival in 1997, further illustrating (and defining) She's divided racial ancestry and anguish. It is ominously relevant that She's white father is dead to her, and that She will always be labeled as black, regardless of how much she attempts to pass as white (Clara Passmore). Kennedy's portrayal of Clara's plight reflects two popular movies of the late 1940s and 1950s, which film-follower

Kennedy doubtless saw, that dealt with miscegenation. *Pinky* (1949), directed by Elia Kazan, and *Imitation of Life* (1959), with Lana Turner, portray young black girls who try to "pass" in the white world but are discovered and ostracized.

No matter how fair-skinned and literate she might be, She/Clara still *"speaks with the soft voice as a Negro school teacher from Savannah would"* (29–30). In an analogous stage direction, Kennedy frames Clara's Bastard's Black Mother standing *"at the gate, watches, and then takes off [her] rose lace dress and black face [beneath her black face is another more pallid Negro face]"* (32). This is precisely what She/Clara attempted to do by pretending she is more white ("pallid") than black. Yet "no matter how pale the face, the body (the entire figure) must read black in a racist culture."[20] As director Susan Booth observed, She/Clara is transcribed by the seer, and not the self (or, more properly, the selves).[21]

She/Clara's fragmentation is symbolized geographically as well as genetically and racially. Place is one of the most consistent signifiers of racial persecution in Kennedy's theater, e.g., an attic, a church, or a classroom. Though many locations are mentioned in *The Owl Answers,* Kennedy basically divides She's various landscapes (psychic, political, racial) into two geographies—an enslaving America, whether it be Jacksonville, Georgia, or a Harlem hotel room, and the valorized places in her British odyssey. These two landscapes represent the two halves of Clara's ancestry—her black heritage and her white, just as Kennedy believed that she was related to the same white ancestors whose descendants lived in Montezuma, Georgia, in the 1930s. Like Aunt Martha, the would-be writer, Adrienne Kennedy was an Anglophile, claiming that the city of London "held a key to my psyche" (*Deadly Triplets,* 105). With funds from a Guggenheim Fellowship (1967) and Rockefeller grants, Kennedy lived in England from 1966 to 1969, and had the experiences Clara could only fantasize about:

> London was a very pleasurable living experience because of the literary community there. I met writers . . . I could write every day. And I met many people in the theater. La MaMa was touring Europe, as well as Joe Chaiken . . . it was a heyday for Americans in London. I met [playwrights] Edward Bond, John Arden . . . all at the Royal Court Theatre's Thursday-afternoon teas.[22]

Kennedy maintained an abiding interest in the city. Not surprisingly, therefore, London also figures prominently in *Funnyhouse of a Negro* and in several of her later plays, most notably the Alexander plays, and in her novel, *Deadly Triplets*. Marc Robinson rightly terms *The Owl Answers* Kennedy's "most sustained play about her attraction to England."[23]

In some of the most lyrical passages in *The Owl Answers*, a calm but delusional Clara recalls London landmarks she visited with her beloved father: "We had a lovely morning, we rose in darkness, took a taxi past Hyde Park through the Marble Arch to Buckingham Palace, we had our morning tea at Lyons then came out to the Tower. We were wandering about the gardens" (30). She/Clara moves symbolically from the darkness of her black self to the sunlit gardens of her fantasized, wished-for white self. Later, She/Clara tells of her plans "to go for lovely walks through Hyde Park, and to innumerable little tearooms with great bay windows and white tablecloths on little white tables and order tea. . . . Then I'll go out to the Tower to see you, my father" (34). With its references to sacrosanct English places and customs, this speech recalls Sarah's obsession with white objects that both declare and demonize her dreams of being white in *Funnyhouse of a Negro*.

Yet when She and her father "had been visiting London together" (33), he died, and with him her hopes of inheriting his stainless white legacy. With Freudian irony, She finds herself "*locked in this tower*" (31), a phallic symbol preventing her from (re)entering the white world, not being allowed to pass on any white blood. The Tower of London has a notorious reputation in British history, and in such plays as Shakespeare's *Henry VI* and *Richard III,* as a cruel and dark prison, a place of execution for political enemies, innocent princes, and other offending royal family members—or for anyone who crossed a British sovereign. Painfully, even She's black family—the Reverend Passmore, the Black Mother, the teachers and principal at her school in Savannah—reinforce the reaction of the punishing white father: "London, who in the hell ever heard of anyone [read: Negro] going to London" (38). This is the response Kennedy herself faced when she expressed her dreams of going to England as an aspiring writer in the 1940s and 1950s.

Jeering at She/Clara, the "white literary fathers" of British culture,[24] Chaucer and Shakespeare, as well as William the Conqueror, her dead father's true ancestors, turn into "the guards in the Tower of London" (30). "She Who Is becomes a prisoner to them." It is a case of "They" versus "She." In her psychic journey, She is shut behind the closed tower doors, entrapped and imprisoned. Shakespeare crosses his hands to her and "*There is a SLAM* as if a great door is being closed" (30). She is thereby denied by three English Williams—the Conqueror; her father, Mattheson; and the quintessential British writer Shakespeare.

Another prisoner of the tower, Anne Boleyn (1507–1536), figures prominently in She's London fantasy/nightmare. Kennedy's interest in Boleyn likewise emerged from her 1960 trip to London. In *People*, Kennedy recorded the shaping influence Henry's executed wife and the mother of Queen Elizabeth I would have on her future work:

> How fascinated by her I was as the Beefeater at the Tower of London told us how Henry VIII had imprisoned her, how she had walked the tower at night and how Henry had beheaded her. Soon Anne would become an image for imprisonment in a play, a confidante whom a character would discuss love and sorrow with. (118)

Visually, the spectral and beheaded Anne Boleyn haunts the tower of She's imagination, an appropriate confidante for the hallucinatory young black woman. Both women have nightmares to tell. Moreover, Anne is one of the three mother figures in She's life—"Bastard's Black Mother who is the Reverend's Wife who is Anne Boleyn." In London, She appeals to Anne, as if to a mother, for help to escape from the tower and to visit her dead father. "I spoke to Anne Boleyn, Dead Father. She knows so much of love and suffering and I believe she is going to try to help me" (33). But, like She/Clara who suffers because of love, Anne is unable to extricate herself or anyone else from patriarchal captivity. The associations between Anne and the Bastard's Black Mother are equally disastrous for She. When She cries for Anne, "*As if trying to bring back Anne Boleyn,*" it is the Bastard's Black Mother who taunts and "*laughs and throws a white bridal bouquet at her.*" She then says, "Clara, I am not Anne. I am the Bastard's Black Mother" (32). The bridal bouquet mocks She's fantasy to be the virginal, marriage-ready daughter of a generous white father.

Just a few minutes earlier on stage, in a gesture even more threatening, Anne *"throws red rice at She Who Is and the Dead Father"* (31), an inversion of a marriage ritual as She is transformed into a bride and her father into a groom. The red rice symbolizes not purity and joy but the stigma of and outrage at She/Clara's blood. A little later, She's other mother, the Reverend's Wife, holds a vial the color of Anne's rice, and exclaims: "These are the fruits of my maidenhead, owl blood Clara who is the Bastard Clara" (32). Symbolically, the red rice thrown by Anne Boleyn stands for the sign of She's sexuality, her tainted ancestry, her doomed blood. Both Anne and the Black Bastard's Mother "represent victims of a male-created hierarchy of sexual power that places blame on them for the 'sins' of bodily lust and racial impurity."[25] Appropriately, Anne reappears in the Harlem hotel room when She recounts her tragedy. And again an importuned Anne changes into the Black Mother, who emphasizes how futile and shameful She's attempts are in casting her tragedy in terms of a prominent white queen from English history.

A significant theme in *The Owl Answers*—and for characters in *Funnyhouse of a Negro* and *The Ohio State Murders* as well—is the self-loathing Clara feels as an aspiring writer through her associations with London: "Now they, my Black Mother and my Father who pretend to be Chaucer, Shakespeare and Eliot and all my beloved English, come to my cell and stare and I can see they despise me and I despise them" (40). Referring to her dead father, She asserts that "you know that England is the home of dear Chaucer, Dickens, and dearest Shakespeare." She then *"takes a sheaf of papers from her notebooks; they fall to the floor."* (33). Clara's papers, the symbol of her vocation to be a writer, fall, dashed like her dreams to connect emotionally and spiritually with these legendary, commanding white authors.

Robert Tener maintains that "She is the composite overlay of her father's cultural heritage and her mother's racial background. Her identity is fragmented because her physical roots are black but almost all of her intellectual (literary) heritage is white."[26] Yet She's intellectual and literary claims are repudiated violently by these authors/fathers. As Clive Barnes stresses, Clara suffers "an intellectual rape"[27] as compellingly tragic as the possibly imagined rape by her white father. In the early 1960s, when Kennedy wrote her first draft of *The Owl Answers,* She/Clara was her surrogate writerly self, as Clara in *Movie Star* would be as well. Paradoxically, with *The Owl Answers* and later with *The Ohio State Murders* and *The Film Club,* Kennedy was vindicated, "taking up residence in a once-forbidden literary history as much as in a city."[28] In the preface to *Deadly Triplets,* Kennedy proudly calls herself an "avid fan" who was "influenced" by such white British mystery writers as Arthur Conan Doyle, Agatha Christie, and especially Daphne du Maurier (vii).

But if London symbolized literary fame for Kennedy and her heroines, it also was the city of nightmares in which Victorian-like terrors and deceptions lurked. As Kennedy herself announced, "The real mystery is perhaps why London has occupied such an important place in my imagination" (*Deadly Triplets,* vii). The reason for her fascination with the city can be found in both her autobiography and its extension into her works. From 1966 to 1969, as we saw, she lived in London on a Guggenheim Fellowship and was "mesmerized" by its theaters, "squares shrouded in mists," palaces, the tower, and "betrayals by archbishops and priests" (*Deadly Triplets,* xi). The city offered beauty, yet boded danger.

It is significant that Kennedy and her heroines both suffer betrayals in London. Like her persona in *Deadly Triplets,* Suzanne Sand, Kennedy saw her project of adopting John Lennon's nonsense books "taken out of [my] hands," suddenly and unexpectedly. While Suzanne's betrayals do not equal the terror of Clara's, they nonetheless capture the deceptions found in Kennedy's mysterious London landscapes. Suzanne falls in love with a handsome British actor, James, who is murdered by his brother, Michael, another actor who takes James's wife and assumes the part he performed in the mystery play *Deadly Triplets,* a drama full of betrayals where three brothers revenge their father's death. Because of her love for James and her letters to him, Suzanne is unsuspectingly involved in this murder plot as well as being the victim of a revenge scheme hatched by her adoptive white sister, Antonia, who concocts gruesome fictions involving a doctored photograph and misleading evidence about the disappearance of Suzanne's fond adoptive white mother, Gina. Through Clara and Suzanne, then, Kennedy the author creates a theater for her own self as she searches for identity as a child of mixed racial heritage. That search symbolically occurs in London, which evoked both dreams and nightmares for Kennedy from her earlier *The Owl Answers* to her later novel *Deadly Triplets.*

Demanding comparison with these London locations and betrayals are the equally punitive and fearsome American landmarks that scar She/Clara's subconscious. In her nightmare world, the two locales tell the same tale of violent subjugation because of her mixed ancestry. In America, as in London, She is shut out, locked up, abused. As the tower door slams, so does the subway door on her journey to Harlem. The two sounds merge in *The Owl Answers*. Retrospectively, She/Clara informs the audience, "I met my father once when my mother took me to visit him and we had to go into the back door of his house" (36), an American indignity that parallels her London fate when she dares to claim being white. As her Dead Father taunts, "So at last you are coming to me, Bastard," we hear the Bastard's Black Mother cruelly exiting "*from the gate . . . and dragging a great dark bed through the gate,*" making sounds that echo tower doors and subway gates slamming shut. Describing another American place of degradation for her, She turns her white father into a rapist.[29] "He came to me in the outhouse, he came to me under the porch" (35). The Dead White Father devolves from the scion of a noble British dynasty into a bigoted plantation owner for whom miscegenation meant power, not love or procreation. The outhouse image above intensifies She's horror at being seen as a black outcast, someone unclean in and for the white world.

Visually and verbally, She's experiences in the Harlem hotel room also recall her entrapment in London and, in fact, may be the result of her London daydreams turning into nightmares. In Harlem, the Negro Man "*tries to kiss her and pin her down on bed. . . . They struggle, he is frightened now. . . . The Negro Man backs out farther out through the gate*" (41–42). Throughout the assault She screeches, howling in agony and dejection. No different than in London, She is the colonized Other, the slave in the outhouse. Calling attention to She's history of woe in geographic and historical terms, Chezia Thompson-Coger intriguingly suggests that "the Bastard is entrapped in the space between worlds as the genetic reminder of European domination and acculturation during and after the Atlantic Slave Trade on the North American continent. This space between worlds in America is shadowy, colored darkness, illuminated by points of light."[30] This is the eerie, liminal place where She suffers in her own psychic film noir, Kennedy's mystery of selves.

Above all of these themes, characters, and places the pervasive symbol of owldom dominates She/Clara's tragedy. The owl is one of the richest, most often discussed symbols in Kennedy's entire canon. Animals, especially ominous birds, frequently inhabit her plays. In *Funnyhouse of a Negro,* ravens swoop forebodingly in Sarah's nightmare. Owls also play a horrific role in *Deadly Triplets,* where Suzanne's spiteful white sister Antonia appears in a "savage" and "frightening" performance piece titled "Birds of Prey" (26). Suzanne recalls that Antonia "sang a description of herself" as an "Arctic owl" who mates "by the light of the midnight sun" and lures larger birds into a terrible death (27). Later, Antonia confesses, "If I did not have my birds, I might murder" (46). Similarly, in *The Owl Answers,* audiences are troubled by the menacing sounds of flapping wings, screeches, and birds caught in cages. Marc Robinson claims that with *A Beast Story* and *A Rat's Mass, The Owl Answers* forms an "animal trilogy."[31] In *The Owl Answers,* the owl is associated with She (it is one of her selves) through a cluster of diverse traditions Kennedy draws upon from African rituals, Greco-Roman myths, and Christianity. The many meanings associated with the owl in her plays and fiction "make it a richly ambiguous metaphor suitable for Kennedy's intentions."[32]

In classical mythology, the owl is linked to Pallas Athena, the "goddess of wisdom and the female domestic arts."[33] Often portrayed alongside Athena, the owl symbolizes insight into self and household. Yet, ironically, for She nothing becomes clear or settled in the "recognition of myself" in her family conflicts. To the contrary, whatever wisdom the owl imparts is damning for She's psychic and family life. In searching for self-knowledge, which the owl traditionally represented, She is plunged into self-destruction, excluded from family. Learning about her tortured genealogy, She is condemned to live through all phases of her tragedy now and forever as an owl. Memory, an attribute also associated with owls, only preserves her pain. Aptly, the Goodman Theatre revival of *The Owl Answers* was set "in the eternal present," underscoring She's ongoing, endless fate as owl. She has to live it, never to be freed or exorcized. The classical virtues, therefore, symbolized by the owl, like the Greco-Roman tradition from which they sprang, ironically are denied to She.

Owldom also represents the sinister, the fatal, the voices of darkness in *The Owl Answers*. The bird is a powerful symbol of She's nightmare, the totem beast of the subway. Linking the owl to miscegenation, Werner Sollors observes that "the owl is secretive. It is only audible at night, yet invisible in the day. Clara's transformation into an owl may thus reenact the father's family relationship that existed only at night."[34] A creature of night and shadows, the owl is frequently associated with death. Amid "life's fitful fevers" and "night's black and deep desires," an owl kills other birds in *Macbeth* (2.4.13). As a minister of darkness, the owl has appropriately been seen as the "transformation of a witch."[35]

The owl also represents the opposite of God's presence. Hearing about her white father's death, She says, "My dead father's bird: God's dove. My father died today" (34). The Reverend Passmore's "canary who is God's dove" is the Holy Spirit, "the white bird," the owl's antithesis. As She ruefully admits, "I call God and the owl answers" (41). In contrast, when God calls His true (white) virginal daughter, He says, "Mary, leave owldom—come into my kingdom" (41). The call of the owl signals She/Clara's abandonment by God. She's spiritual legacy, therefore, is taken away, marked by her transformation into an owl. Blasphemously, She even calls the Negro Man in Harlem "God." Robert Tener appropriately links such abandonment to Clara's race. "The ominous inference is that Christianity as a religion of white men is not psychologically or historically suited to She."[36] Rosemary Curb argues that She's "corrupted state of owldom is associated with black female carnality [which] inevitably leads to death." According to a condemning white Christianity, She inherited that carnality, her "evil, sensual, bestial side," from her mother, the black cook.[37] She/Clara's ultimate sin, then, and the signifier of her owldom, is that she is black. Being trapped in owldom, therefore, underscores She's loss of salvation because of her race. Further reinforcing the damnation shared by owls and black women, She's Black Mother asserts, "There is a way from owldom" (41), and then stabs herself with a butcher knife, the ultimate sin of despair against God's mercy and forgiveness.

The owl's color is also symbolic of She's condemned mixed heritage. Contrasting the white purity of Mary with She/Clara's ancestry, the Reverend's Wife describes She as "owl blood Clara who is the Bastard Clara Passmore to whom we gave our name, see the Owl blood, that is why I cry when I see Marys, cry for their deaths, Owl Mary Passmore" (32). Unlike Mary—the Blessed Virgin—She bears the taint of owl, not pure, blood, as the offspring of a white father and black mother. Similarly, in *Deadly Triplets,* the revengeful white Antonia includes a "Pet Tawny [yellowish brown] Owl" among her avian menagerie, no doubt alluding to her adopted sister Suzanne, a child of mixed blood. Appropriately then, the owl is described as yellow in *The Owl Answers*. She refers to the owl that haunts her (as one of her selves) as "feathered, great hollow-eyed with yellow skin and yellow eyes, the flying bastard" (41). E. Barnsley Brown links this color symbolism to She/Clara as the "inscription of mixed-blooded, yellow-skinned mulatto."[38] Kennedy recalls that her mother as a young girl mistakenly walked "on the white side of town" and was attacked by a white man who called to her, "You little yellow bastard, what are you doing here?"[39] This color symbolism lies behind the Black Bastard Mother personifying and physicalizing her daughter. "That's why you are an owl" (32).

Going beyond mere personification, Kennedy actually turns She and her Black Mother into owls. When She/Clara speaks to her, the Black Mother *"remains seated like an owl"* (34) and later "puts owl feathers about her" (37). Visually linking herself to the sinful bird, the lost Black Mother prepares her bed/altar with owl feathers. But on Kennedy's multivalent stage, the Black Mother, like her daughter, becomes a sacrificial victim on an altar that represents a perverse white Christianity. Tragically assimilated into owldom, She herself *"screeches like an owl"* (42) and *"suddenly looks like an owl"* at the end of the play. One critic ingeniously suggests a pun on She's own name "She Who Is—*Whooo*,"[40] echoing the owl's call.

She/Clara's denigration and metamorphosis into an owl is one of the cruelest fates in all of Kennedy's canon. Her owldom, like Sister's transformation into a rat in *A Rat's Mass*, dehumanizes her. The fact that She's utterances are reduced to the repetition of the harrowing "Ow . . . oww" (42) charts the depths into which She descends into the hell of owldom. In one of the most alarming transformations in Kennedy's theater,

Clara "passes" from being a gifted young black woman into a nightmarish animal, an owl. Once a highly articulate student and promising writer, She is cruelly erased by a society that outlaws her beauty and her voice, much the same way that Philomela (the raped sister in Ovid's *Metamorphoses*) was reduced to silence by having her tongue cut out. But in the white classical world, Philomela was transformed into a regal nightingale, not a cursed owl, She's sad fate.

A Beast Story

Not as fully developed as *Funnyhouse of a Negro* or *The Owl Answers, A Beast Story,* nonetheless, is a necessary chapter in Kennedy's exploration of the fragmented self. In *A Beast Story,* we find another black family who lives in a perpetual nightmare. "In reality," they live in the "gloomy house of a minister in a drab Midwestern city" (32), but on Kennedy's surrealistic stage, the minister/father is transformed into Beast Man, the wife and mother becomes Beast Woman, and their daughter is Beast Girl. The fourth resident is Dead Human, whom Beast Girl married but murdered. Sharing horrors and lines with Beast Man, Beast Woman, and Dead Human, Beast Girl and her traumas are thus relayed through the multiple identities of bride, father, mother, and husband. As in *Funnyhouse of a Negro,* Beast Man has raped his wife and wants to do the same to his daughter. The prototypical Kennedy mother, Beast Woman *"wander[s] through the rooms"* and goes through "endless wakeful fits" (38). Both parents were saddened by their daughter marrying. In a foreboding similarity to *Sun,* Kennedy's eulogy for Malcolm X, "a black sun floated over the altar" and "a crow flew through an open window" (34). Amid these grotesqueries, Beast Girl murders her child and then smothers Dead Human, who rocks their dead baby in the attic. At the end of the play, she tries to ax her father to death and then kills herself. Beast Girl asks the central question of the play, "Could I have been human?" (35).

The answers to that question constitute many of Kennedy's themes in *A Beast Story*. This family has turned into beasts because of the sins that haunt Kennedy's canon—religious hypocrisy, violence, sexual trauma, rejection of the daughter, child-killing, and the inevitable onset of madness through guilt as punishment and through nightmares. But unlike Clara of *The Owl Answers,* the girl in *A Beast Story* is victimized less by white prejudice than by her own family's torments and communal hallucinations. "They seem bound to an endless cycle of mutual recriminations."[41] Because of these crimes, she and her family enter "Dragon Country," Tennessee Williams's phrase for the psychic territory where compassion, dignity, and love are hunted down and destroyed.[42] The leading citizen of that dragon country is Beast Man, who tells his daughter, "I am more than your father. I am an accomplice to your fate. I believe in the connection too of dreams of dark winter nights. I believe in the joining of nightmares and visions" (41).

In this particular nightmare vision, then, bestiality (rather than a funnyhouse or the Tower of London and subway of *The Owl Answers*) controls and structures Kennedy's setting and imagery. Unlike Aesop's fables, where human beings learn lessons about being human through events that befall animals, in *A Beast Story* humans learn how to act like beasts, turning home, selves, relationships, and even religion into the inhuman. Kennedy frighteningly fuses the domestic and the bestial: "My father comes to the door of my room, smiles, stopping in the hallway. . . . My mother sits staring at a blank wall, brushing her beast hair. . . . Our supper bones are on the floor, noises in the forest" (36). The Beast family share visions, images, and blood-soaked horrors.

Multiplying the ravens, owl-like creatures, and rats from *Funnyhouse of a Negro, The Owl Answers,* and *A Rat's Mass, A Beast Story* contains Kennedy's most extreme menagerie of hideous animality. Crows, toads, jackals, mice, all amid "floating images" of the dead, are seen and heard everywhere, even hovering above the house. Toads were one of the cursed beasts that rained upon Pharaoh's family (Exodus 8:2–8), and jackals prey upon the dead, Apocalyptic contexts within which *A Beast Story* can be read. "Outside wolves and bears" search for victims. "Beasts stare into the windows" (38), claims Beast Girl, and inside "animals wander through our house" (37). A "giant toad croaking" ends the play. "I am trapped in this beast house" (40), Dead Human cries, yet the play reveals how the terror from beasts outside is equaled and replicated by the bestiality within family and self. The terrorized become the source of terror.

The father's ministerial missions are unholy, bestial. A hypocritical pastor like the Reverend Passmore, Beast Man "took on the appearance of an animal in his black preacher's suit" (36). He says of his wife that she "had snatched my collar. I walked to my table, sat down and opened the Bible. I had raped my wife" (36). Sanctimoniously, he sings without stopping, a reference to his sermonizing self-righteousness. But "he sings a beast song" (39), not Godly hymns. An ominous sign, "His face exudes a yellow light"; yet even more threateningly the "sky turns black" (39), symbolizing the perversity of his religion. Through lustful designs on his daughter, this father destroys her marriage, an action aptly described through nonhuman references. His dead son-in-law tells Beast Girl, "He was the beast that sent you from me" (35). Because of her father, Beast

Girl loses her innocence and suffers the loss of her humanity. As Dead Human tells her, "Your hair grown, eyes turned beast yellow, the toad knew, the toad has always known. The first night of our marriage you fled from our bed. I found you, face ravaged, sitting in your father's room, staring at the candles. Afterwards they made you kill my baby" (35).

In terms of Kennedy's beast metaphors, the sins of the father are visited upon the child and, in turn, her child, three generations deep. Kennedy's canon bleeds with infanticide—hiding dead rat babies in an attic reflects the generational curses in *A Rat's Mass*, and twin baby daughters are murdered in *The Ohio State Murders*. Violating a family member's human dignity and sexuality, whether physically or psychically, puts a generation at risk of descending into a supernatural world where human beings see themselves and others trapped as beasts. "Freud is always implicit if not explicit . . . in Kennedy's fantasies."[43] Characteristically, a confused sexual identity is tied to a confused spiritual one in Kennedy's plays. The violation of Beast Girl by her beast father and the symbolic destruction of her child—or the child who was (within) her—have overwhelming theological implications. When people act like and answer to the names of beasts, we are thrust again into the prophetic world of the Apocalypse. In this typical Kennedy territory, young black women and children are branded for life because of violence and madness. Symbolically, Kennedy links their descents into bestiality with the evils of moving to the city. Recalling an earlier life, Beast Woman cries, "Our ravaged beast faces . . . the jackals, the toad and the mice are glad. The toad remembers when we were southern Negroes who came to the city" (37). From rural innocence, they have arrived and are transformed into beasts in one of the cities in Bezique.

In their bestiality, the family destroys the sacred rituals and institutions that have forged the bonds of humanity. As in *The Owl Answers* and *A Rat's Mass,* religious rituals—marriage, birth—are turned upside down, travestied in the nightmare arena of *A Beast Story.* Beast Girl's own birth is surrounded with evil omens. As Beast Woman says, "I went into labor at my dead sister's funeral" (36). Invoking images of Christ's nativity, Beast Girl recalls, "My father built a crib. How he loved me, saw me in the crib, circled by the golden aureole" (37). Yet "black shadows were etched under her mother's eyes," canceling any possibility of a happy birth or happy childhood. Killing her own child with "quinine and whiskey" (35), an absurd and fatal substitute for mother's milk, further links Beast Girl and her family with child killers, beasts. Speaking of his marriage, Beast Man tells his wife, "You spoke of death at our wedding. I did not answer. Was I speaking of death or was it God?" (37). At his daughter's wedding, disgusting animals—toads and crows—officiate. Her mother gives her an ax as a wedding present to "preserve her innocence." Not surprisingly, she runs from her husband, as her mother did from her father, fleeing from memories of struggles and "sheets of blood" (36). As if Kennedy's script were haunted by *Othello,* where the black husband smothers his white wife, Desdemona, who fleetingly comes to life but then dies, Beast Girl "takes a pillow, never taking her eyes from" her husband, "smothers him with all her strength. He moves fiercely as though he will spring up but instead totters backward. He holds out his hand, trying to reach her" (41). Dead Human, with his compassionate feelings, evokes the victimized Desdemona in *Othello.*

Along with many other Kennedy heroines, Beast Girl "lives in the shadows" (38)—literally, given the subdued, yellow lighting on stage, and psychologically, as she battles ghosts within and outside of herself. "Dust fills the room" (36), ambiguously referring to death as well as cobwebs concealing hideous family secrets. She lives in a Kennedyesque nightmare world of blood, axes, dead babies, and husbands damned to the attics of the living dead.

CHAPTER 4

Black Rats and White Dogs

A Rat's Mass and A Lesson in Dead Language

A Rat's Mass

Written in 1963, *A Rat's Mass* was first performed by the Boston Theater Company in 1966 and again at La MaMa Experimental Theatre Company in October 1969. The play was later set to music by jazz composer Cecil Taylor; this piece was titled "A Rat's Mass/Procession." *A Rat's Mass* is a play of initiation acted out through Kennedy's surrealistic animal rituals. A horrifying one-act play, *A Rat's Mass* stages traumatic childhood memories through fantastic images, places, and characters. Rooted in Kennedy's subconscious, *A Rat's Mass* grew out of a dream she had on a train ride from Paris to Rome: "I was being pursued by red, bloodied rats. It was very powerful dream, and when I woke up the train had stopped in the Alps. It was night. . . . It was a crucial night in my life. So I was just haunted by that image for years."[1] She further explained that this dream occurred about the time her brother Cornell was in a fatal automobile accident.

Appropriately, *A Rat's Mass* centers on Brother Rat (Blake) and Sister Rat (Kay), "two pale Negro children," who lose their innocence, identities, and, most sadly, their holiness because in their hysteria they believe that a white neighbor girl, Rosemary, forces them to commit incest in a playground. But the horrors of the playground, like those in Sarah's room in *Funnyhouse of a Negro,* are recycled in a theater of the mind as the children suffer from the guilt and madness that surround the memory of a hidden sin. "Did you tell?" asks Brother (50). Ironically, their crime occurs on "Memorial Day," according to Sister Rat (48). Kennedy's brother and sister trapped in madness demand comparison with Tennessee Williams's brother and sister, Felice and Clare, in *The Two-Character Play* (1967).

Kennedy saturates *A Rat's Mass* with their interior voices, relaying images of blood, bombs, dead babies, cats with sunflower seeds in their mouths, dead rats, and perverse religious rites. She conflates the Holocaust, blitzkrieg, and Nazis—events and people from World War II, when she and her brother grew up in Cleveland—with the epoch of such ancestral white heroes as Julius Caesar into a terrifying present, a simultaneity. In *June and Jean in Concert,* based on *People Who Led to My Plays,* Kennedy recalls thinking during World War II that "if Hitler comes to Cleveland and we resist, will we be beaten and sent to a concentration camp?" (246). June has nightmares of Nazi aggression. After seeing "*Hitler's Children* with my brother and the kids from next door, we were very upset that Bonita Granville . . . was beaten by the SS, the German officers" (246). Like June, the siblings of *A Rat's Mass* have their personal horrors from racial oppression historicized and intensified through allusions to similar crimes in World War II. Brother and Sister Rat are holocausted souls in an allegorized theater of trauma.

As in Kennedy's other plays, *A Rat's Mass* has a highly symbolic setting—a house that represents several psychically rooted and linked locations. As Jeanie Forte notes, Kennedy's plays present a "terrain in flux," just like her characters' lives and minds.[2] The rooms in *A Rat's Mass* recall Kennedy's childhood home in Cleveland, which also figured in the dream that inspired the play. Thinking of her dead brother, Kennedy confessed, "evoked an almost unreal memory of when we were children we used to play in the attic and there used to be a closet in the floor . . . I didn't like to go up there by myself because I would imagine there would be something in the closet."[3] In *A Rat's Mass,* she opens that closet door, and out spill the horrors she and her brother feared.

In archetypically Jungian terms, a house symbolizes female nurturing, safety, and motherhood. But the shadowy rooms in *A Rat's Mass* become the site of childhood nightmares. Pointing to this nightmarish quality, Arthur Sainer found that in a 1969 production the actors "endowed the characters with a sense of somnambulists whose present condition consists of recalling in agony the observations of the past."[4] The interiority of these characters' lives, and those of their oppressors, is physicalized through attics and closets, powerful symbols for psychic spaces and for the forbidden. Rooms and spaces in *A Rat's Mass* are loaded with charged prepositions. The children "hide *in* the attic like rats" (50). "Everyday I look *under* our house to see who is listening," says Sister (50). "*Within* our house is a great slide" (48), they both intone. The use of *in, under,* and *within* transports audiences from physical to psychic spaces in Kennedy's attic closet.

The setting captures the children's enduring trauma as victims of an institutional white theology that condemns them for being black, as it does Clara in *The Owl Answers.* Once their home was a place of holiness and innocence—"we lived in a Holy Chapel with parents and Jesus, Joseph, Mary, our Wise Men and our Shepherd" (48), the sacred figures of the crèche also found in *A Lesson in Dead Language*. But this house becomes unholy ground, a cathedral for rats, mocking the sanctified spaces of a church with a *"red carpet runner"* (47), candles, and an altar. The "rat cathedral," a perversion of a place of worship and forgiveness, fittingly represents the white establishment's punishment of the children for wanting to be both white and holy, and for concealing their sin, as Clara also tragically found out in St. Paul's Cathedral in *The Owl Answers*.

Kennedy emphasizes the architectural features of the house —attic, beams, rafters, basement, giant slide—as distorted and dislocated spaces, grotesque inversions of the children's once-sinless home. The red runner leading to the altar in a church, as in Jean and June's holy procession for their concert before their congregation, is perverted in *A Rat's Mass* as an aisle of blood or pathway to execution in the chapel and on the playground (53). The rat's chapel corresponds to a sacrilegious funnyhouse for the children's victimized spirits. Imprisoned in this chapel, they are excluded from sacred spaces just as they were evicted from the "place of white birch trees" (49) intoned in the play's poetic litanies of horror. Their rat chapel is simultaneously a prison, an execution chamber, an abortion clinic, and a state hospital, all of them covered in blood. In the children's hysteria, Sister Rat goes away to "State Hospital" after the traumatic birth of her rat baby, but psychically that madhouse or hell is within her own rat cathedral. Horrors occupy boundless space.

Kennedy's rat symbolism is multivalent. Visually and verbally, the children are transformed into rats—Brother has a rat's head and tail and Sister a rat's belly for the child she conceives supposedly through incest, features emphasized in productions of the play. They both have *"rat-like movements,"* conceive a baby like a rat, see dying rats everywhere, and walk over rat graves. Even their language sounds like rats gnawing; they "become more rat-like as the play progresses."[5] Portraying the children as rats empowers the white world to dehumanize them as unnatural, beyond redemption. The rat also symbolizes racial roles that society assigns to black children, stigmatizing them as the grotesque Other. White society thereby perpetuates its own segregationist racial expectations. Blackness is equated with loathsomeness, the ugly, the nonhuman, being fit for extermination, as Sarah in *Funnyhouse of a Negro* laments after her mother "was raped by a wild black beast." Black is evil. Historically, rats, brown and black, were thought to carry disease, a point the Nazis made when they metamorphosed the Jews, their racial enemies, into swarming rats in Joseph Goebbels's fascist propaganda films of the 1930s. In the 1960s, when Kennedy wrote *A Rat's Mass,* some El Paso, Texas, exterminators dehumanized Mexican Americans, their racial Other, by portraying them on billboards and in newspaper ads as large sombrero-wearing rodents with Hispanic features and names. Kennedy's animal symbolism makes painfully visual the horror and absurdity of such vile racial characterizations.

If ratness dehumanizes Brother and Sister, it also demonizes them. Their transformation is a reflection of and punishment for their sexual/racial sins. As Rosemary Curb usefully points out, "The partial metamorphoses are symbolically appropriate since Blake willed the sin which Rosemary counseled, and Kay exhibits it in her belly."[6] The children's transmogrification into rats strips away their dignity and their identities, leaving only self-hatred. Their guilt is inescapable. Sister pleads in vain with Brother that "we must rid our minds of my rat's belly" (53). Transformed into rats, the children are cast into a spiritual darkness with no hope for escape. Brother repeatedly fears a "dark sun" (52), the death of spring, the onset of winter. This reference only reinforces the idea that rats were, as bearers of plagues, regarded as punishments sent to earthly sinners by an angry God.

"Atone us" (50), the children cry. But they cannot be pardoned, no matter what, by the condemning white world they hoped to join. Through a collage of religious references, Kennedy hauntingly reveals the children's fates as if they were being exorcized. "I am damned," cries Brother for his presumptive act of incest. The children as rats suffer "the mystery of the isolated soul recurring in Kennedy's plays."[7] "Deliver us unto your descendents," they plead to Rosemary, their Italian friend (50), who loathes and betrays them. Thinking he can be saved, a deceived Brother Rat cries to Rosemary, "I am a descendant of the Pope and Julius Caesar and the Virgin Mary" (49). Brother asks the same question that Clara Passmore does in *The Owl Answers:* "I am almost white, am I not" (31). And as the white characters in *The Owl Answers* respond, "If you are his ancestor why are you a Negro?" (30), so does Rosemary speaking of her ancestor Caesar. The children are thus excluded from the white world of history and theology.

So heinous is their crime that they are abandoned even by the Procession of Mary, Jesus, Joseph, Two Wise Men, and the Shepherd. "Goodbye, Kay and Blake. We are leaving you" (51), the Procession taunts, an action Matthew Roudané labels a "negative epiphany."[8] Intensifying the children's forlorn spiritual state, the Procession leaves "because it was Easter" (51), the ultimate Christian feast of redemption. Theologically, spring is the time of hope, rebirth, and salvation, which Brother and Sister thought they were to possess but now can never hope to attain. According to Rosemary, "You must damn last spring in your heart. You will never see last spring again" (51). In one of Kennedy's most caustic attacks on a bigoted white Christianity, the procession at the end of *A Rat's Mass* is transformed into Nazis who shoot the children, illustrating how the sacred is perfidiously co-opted by racial politics.

The grotesque religious symbolism at the heart of Kennedy's play coalesces as the children offer up a Mass in their chapel. As Clive Barnes claims, the play is a "parody mass"; it is also a surrealistic "kind of black spiritual."[9] The religious allusions and events in *A Rat's Mass* perversely mirror parts of the traditional Roman Catholic Mass, emphasizing how far from grace Brother and Sister have fallen because of prejudice and self-hatred. A phantasmagoric Jesus, Mary, Joseph, Wise Men, and Shepherd process through the chapel, but the dimly lit chapel is dislocated; it is a rat chapel in a nightmare where a "rat's mass" is frighteningly offered. Brother and Sister are cast as the celebrants, fittingly, with a congregation of rats before them: "Now there are rats in the church books behind every face in the congregation" (49). Throughout the play, Brother and Sister kneel, rise, kneel again, and pray, grotesquely imitating the rituals of the community of the faithful at Holy Mass.

Parodying these rituals, Kennedy's play can be interpreted in terms of specific parts of the Mass. The Catholic Mass begins with the Penitential Rite, including an examination of conscience and prayers for forgiveness: "I confess to you, Almighty God, and to you my brothers and sisters that I have sinned through my own fault, in my thoughts, in my words, in what I have done and in what I have failed to do. And I ask you, my brothers and sisters, to pray for me." As the audience is hurled into a desecration of this penitential rite, Kennedy literalizes the "brother" and "sister" of the Mass by focusing incessantly on the children's guilt. Unlike the Mass, though, the rat's mass does not lead to or promise forgiveness. Nor are Brother and Sister Rat blessed through the Gloria, the next part of the Mass, a highly lyrical, even mystic praise of God that is often sung but is always omitted during the penitential seasons of Lent and Advent. It is worth noting that no part of *A Rat's Mass* alludes to the Gloria, since the children live in a perpetual state of penance and punishment. The Liturgy of the Word—the good news of the Gospel—follows the Gloria in the Mass, but, again, the word is deadly in a rat's mass: "The Nazis have invaded our house" (48).

At the center of the Mass is the Liturgy of the Eucharist, the preparation of the altar and the transubstantiation of bread and wine into the sacred body and blood of Christ. Kennedy prepares the rat's altar with blood and terror through repeated references to the red runner. Further parodying the preparation of the altar for the Eucharist, "*Rosemary comes down the red aisle in her Holy Communion dress*" (50). Paradoxically, *A Rat's Mass* uses Brother and Sister's blood to transform them into rats. "Every sister bleeds and every brother has made her bleed. The Communion wine" (49). Perverting the sacrament of the Eucharist, Brother and Sister eat petals, "great gnawed sunflowers" (52), an unholy communion that leads not to being more Christ-like and gaining eternal life, but, on the contrary, to sickness, death, and damnation. The fact that these petals are found in the mouths of winter "dying and grey cats" (47) may also be an allusion to Grimalkin, one of the Witches' familiars in *Macbeth* (1.1.9), another grey cat. In terms of Kennedy's animal symbolism, cats chase, kill, and eat rats. Ironically, the grey cats receive communion while Brother and Sister Rat eat gnawed petals. The Prayer of Intercession after Holy Communion is twisted into this petition from the lips of Brother and Sister, "God we ask you to stop throwing dead rat babies" (52), referring to the death of black children psychically (and physically) destroyed by the prejudice of a white religion. Rather than concluding with a blessing as at Mass, the play ends with curses from Rosemary, "Perhaps you can put a bullet in your head" (51) and "My greatest grief was your life together" (53).

The architect of the children's harrowing experiences is Rosemary, the Italian-American girl who once befriended and sang with the children, and "taught us Latin and told us stories of Italy" (49). Brother Rat was once even in love with her. Rosemary comes right out of Kennedy's biography. In "Secret Paragraphs about My Brother," she recalls that a neighborhood girl by that name "married" her brother "when he was six and I was nine." Coming "to the edge of the field of weeds," Kennedy saw "Rosemary and my brother standing before a boy I'd never seen. Rosemary was in her communion dress . . . when my brother came home toward dark . . . [he said] 'Don't tell mother and daddy. I'm married'" (237). But in *A Rat's Mass* Brother goes on no "honeymoon" with Rosemary. Like Edmund Spenser's Fidessa/Duessa in book 1 of the *Faerie Queene,* Rosemary is the demonic woman masquerading as a model of piety. As the saint/whore, she embodies the horrors of racial prejudice reflected in the childhood world of a bigoted, institutional theology. Surrounding herself with imagery of a segregated white Christianity, Rosemary, with no doctrinal basis, wickedly declares that "colored" children cannot be Catholic (49).

Her name blasphemously suggests the Rose of Sharon (Christ) and Mary (the Blessed Virgin), yet she travesties the scriptural love of both. Stressing the sacrilegious nature of the character, in the 1969 production of *A Rat's Mass* at La Mama,

Brother and Sister "first knelt to, and then exorcized, the destructive influence of this white idol."[10] In a University of Louisville production of *A Rat's Mass* on 16 November 2001, the actor playing Rosemary was sacrilegiously propped up on the altar and dressed like the Virgin Mary, all in white.[11] Rosemary's name also recalls the flower for remembrance in *Hamlet* (4.5.175), but, again ironically, this Rosemary brings not happy memories but nightmares. She wears a spotless Communion dress (echoing Kennedy's childhood memories of their neighbor Rosemary), while Sister Rat's, not surprisingly, appears ratlike for her unholy communion. However, the most surrealistic reminders of Rosemary's Fidessa/Duessa role are the worms in her hair. They suggest Medusa's poisoned snakes, but they also point to the snake that betrayed Adam and Eve in the Garden. The fact that Rosemary's father owns a grape arbor that the children once visited contributes to such a reading. Allusions to a prelapsarian Eden as well as Communion wine may be found in this perverse white arbor. The vineyard may also recall "Mr. Bertiloni's grape arbor" in the Mount Pleasant section of Cleveland that June (Kennedy's fictive self) mentions in *June and Jean in Concert* (243).

Given her father's grape arbor and Brother Rat's being in love with her, Rosemary further typifies both temptress and destroyer. Sexually, she can again be likened to the malevolent Duessa whore, the dangerous, smiling harlot of the book of Proverbs (7:10–27). In the London production of *A Rat's Mass* in May 1970, Rosemary was portrayed as a "white-laced patroness who changes into a death's head whore."[12] Moreover, when she is seated on top of the slide watching the incestuous children whom she seduced, Rosemary "occupies the masculine and even pornographic position of ownership of the gaze and the act."[13] She anticipates the vindictive white coed Patricia "Bunny" Manley, who torments Suzanne Alexander in *The Ohio State Murders*. But Brother Blake and Sister Kay never escape from their haunted years to attend college. The Nazi/procession execution squad makes them realize that, like the innocent, pre–World War II America, they "weren't safe long" (48).

A Lesson in Dead Language

A Lesson in Dead Language, which premiered in 1964 and was subsequently staged at the Royal Court Theatre in London in 1968, continues Kennedy's exploration of the terror involved in learning what it means to be a black child. It is helpful to read *A Rat's Mass* and *A Lesson in Dead Language* as companion works—one-act memory plays about the cruel initiations black children undergo as they move from sexual innocence into the nightmare world of guilt. Both plays incorporate frightening animals—dogs and rats—as agents of a punishing white society. Moreover, both plays are structured around issues of gender, sexuality, and religion. In *A Lesson in Dead Language,* seven black girls are tragically inducted into womanhood after their first menstruations by a white world that despises their power to reproduce. The children in *A Rat's Mass* also participate in an imagined sexual initiation ritual—intercourse/incest—for which they, too, are terrifyingly spurned and damned by the white establishment. The settings for both plays are appropriate for a child's traumatized memory. *A Lesson in Dead Language* takes place in a grotesque classroom, while *A Rat's Mass* is set in a childhood home transformed into a torture-chamber cathedral. Like Sarah in *Funnyhouse of a Negro,* the children in these plays are besieged by cataclysmic memories associated with physical/psychic spaces.

But the set in *A Lesson in Dead Language* is no ordinary classroom. It is harrowingly surrealistic, making learning an exercise in racial shame. This schoolroom has three blackboards —powerful icons for the racialized parameters of Kennedy's stage—where *"statues of Jesus, Joseph, Mary, two Wise Men and a shepherd are on a ridge around the room"* (43). Emerging from the dark shadows of Kennedy's unbounded unconscious, the schoolroom in *A Lesson in Dead Language* is a place of ghastly, grisly horrors. This classroom of the mind is far different from the classrooms in which Kennedy excelled. A biographically pertinent detail is that Kennedy majored in elementary education at Ohio State University and intended, like her mother, to teach in the Cleveland public schools. Kennedy, a master teacher, has been devoted to helping her students produce excellent work at Yale, Princeton, Harvard, and the University of California at Berkeley. She insists that her students keep a journal—"I want to try to free the unconscious. I'm a great believer in diaries."[14]

Dominating this room is a huge White Dog who drills the seven black girls on their Latin lessons. Her whiteness, like that of Sarah's white makeup, is a sign of decay and death. *"Costumed like a dog from the waist up"* (43), the White Dog is like a satyr—a lustful creature who looked like a human from the waist up but like an animal from the waist down—but inverted. In the girls' nightmare lesson, the White Dog demonstrates a human, rational sensibility being turned into that of an animal; moreover, the dog's costume again exemplifies how identities are fragmented and distorted in the funnyhouse of Kennedy's imagination. She imperiously orders the girls to write on "imaginary tablets," answer her questions, *"go stiffly to the boards"* and write *"I killed"* (44), hang their heads, and stand in shame with their backs to the audience. Victims of their blackness, the girls wear white organdy dresses streaked with blood, familiarly horrific costumes in Kennedy's plays, as we saw in *Funnyhouse of a Negro* and *A Rat's Mass.*

As in her other works, Kennedy links black women's sexuality with bloody crimes, especially assassinations, in *A Lesson in Dead Language.* Recall that one of Sarah's nightmare tormentors in *Funnyhouse of a Negro* is the assassinated Patrice Lumumba, with his bloody, cracked skull. In *A Lesson in Dead Language,* the White Dog accuses the girls of killing Caesar, and the repeated references to his assassination may stem from Kennedy's fascination with Joseph Mankiewicz's 1953 film *Julius Caesar,* featuring Marlon Brando as Brutus, whose picture from the film she included in *People.* Kennedy's knowledge and reinterpretation of Julius Caesar's assassination also surely emerge from her having studied the classics in high school. Branding these seven black girls as conspirators, the White Dog insists that their bleeding started "at the Ides of March" (44), when "Caesar [bleeds] too" (46), and concludes, "Since no one knows, then we all bleed and continue to bleed" (45). Explicating the "bleeding, menstruating, sexual initiation, or deflowering" in *A Lesson in Dead Language,* Rosemary Curb argues "that the blood-soaked dresses may suggest sexual violation but more likely menses" and believes the lesson shows an "unusual chain of seminal causality leading to the pupils' collective guilt as conspirators plotting to overthrow the white European ancestral authority."[15] Caesar is the archetype for such authority; his assassination was seen as a defining political, even theological, event in Western history. His murder can be connected to the "photographs of Roman ruins" in Sarah's room in *Funnyhouse of a Negro,* which also reveal icons of a white, classical culture mocking and indicting her for being black.

Further stressing the girls' crime against a white phallic figure, the White Dog insists that they repeat lines about the omens surrounding Caesar's death, including "Calpurnia dreamed a pinnacle was tumbling down" (46). Interestingly enough, Caesar refused to listen to his third wife, Calpurnia, just as the world of white power refuses to listen to the seven black girls —a case of transcultural misogyny and marginalization. The White Dog's lesson about Caesar demands comparison with similar scenes in Shakespeare's *The Merry Wives of Windsor* (4.1) and *Titus Andronicus* (4.1), where Latin lessons become occasions to reflect on social and sexual crimes. Another apt point of comparison is with Eugene Ionesco's *The Lesson,* the play in the tradition of the theater of the absurd that has been frequently cited as a source for Kennedy's work.

In terms of the overall theme in *A Lesson in Dead Language,* though, critics have primarily focused on the politics of womanhood. As Claudia Barnett claims, "The girls' crime is simply that they have been born; their punishment is that they may give birth themselves."[16] Their biological history is inextricably linked to haunting color-coded symbols, painted in vivid shades of blood red, white (again, as fur), lemon yellow, and grass green. Throughout the incantatory dialogue, this color symbolism animates Kennedy's plotless nightmare, as exemplified by these lines the girls speak in unison: "I bleed, Teacher, I bleed. It started when my white dog died. It was a charming little white dog. He ran beside me in the sun when I played a game of lemons on the green grass. And it started when I became a woman" (44). White color symbolism also marks the accusation that the girls killed the sun and Christ, additional references to a purity that white society invokes as its exclusive signifier.

Through such pervasive color imagery, Kennedy mourns the lost happiness of girlhood in deeply ritualistic terms, dredging up mythic memories of doomed innocence, threatened fertility, and racial guilt. She describes the onset of their bleeding using a characteristically symbolic landscape mirroring the girls' psychic and sexual states as they follow orders from and are indicted by their White Dog teacher. In referring to their game of lemons on the green grass, Kennedy again evokes the garden, a prelapsarian safe zone, a pastoral landscape of the mind contrasting with the martinet terrors of the classroom. The girls lived in this Edenic world of cool, green thoughts, sunshine, and play before their menses and the possibility of laboring birth transported them into black womanhood. This was the world of idyllic, holy childhood also envisioned in *A Rat's Mass* before the children fell from grace. The girls would agree with Brother Rat, "If only we could go back to our childhood" (51).

Their "little white dog," in contrast with their punishing teacher, the big White Dog, has been seen as their "imagined scapegoat."[17] But such a reading is only partially accurate; much more is at work here. The little dog stands for the gamboling innocence, the girls' comforting paschal friend. In his company, they are bloodless and pure; the animal, symbolic of a happy childhood, does not force them into the world of blood and the trauma of black womanhood. But this little white dog may also signify the false security of childhood's illusory dreams and hopes. Possibly, too, it alludes to another little white dog representing idyllic dreaming—Sheba in William Inge's *Come Back, Little Sheba* (1950), a highly popular play that Kennedy, as a keen cultural observer of the 1950s, in all likelihood knew. For her frumpy, unfulfilled owner, Lola, Sheba crystallized romantic fancies that had to end for Lola's life to continue realistically. At the end of Inge's play, Lola confesses: "I couldn't find Little Sheba . . . she was lying in the middle of a field . . . dead. . . .

That sweet little puppy . . . her curly white fur all smeared with mud . . . I'm not going to call her anymore."[18] Like Sheba, the little white dog in *A Lesson in Dead Language* must die for the girls to enter womanhood, though their transition is far more terrifying than Lola's into adult, wedded maturity.

The game of lemons also symbolizes the physiology of womanhood that is a trope in Kennedy's surrealistic childhood memory play. Lemons, the color of golden sunshine, connote freshness and innocence, yet the black girls' game with them ritualistically occurs on the very day the little white dog died. Their childhood games—vulnerable, prepubescent, and benign—are replaced by bloody nightmares and punishments when they become women in the eyes of a White Dog–dominated society. Frolics (the game of lemons with the little white dog) turn into fury because of white prejudice and fear of black femininity/womanhood. Anatomically, the lemons might also be a figuration of the girls' ovaries, and the bitter taste of womanhood before them.[19] Every symbol in Kennedy's work is multivalent, admitting varied readings. Her plays are constructed out of "a chain of linked images,"[20] as the grass, lemons, dogs, blood, and white dresses illustrate.

A Lesson in Dead Language, like other Kennedy plays, also incorporates venerated religious symbols, intensifying the sexual pain these young girls experience in maturing into black women. As in *A Rat's Mass* and *The Owl Answers,* Kennedy embeds Roman Catholic rituals within her script of frightening biology, asking audiences to trowel through layers of allusion and desecration as she delves into the unconscious. According to director Gaby Rodgers, who collaborated with Kennedy by including the Stations of the Cross in the set for the Theatre Genesis's production of *A Lesson in Dead Language* in 1971,

Kennedy "loved the ceremonies of the church [but] there was also fear" in them for her.[21] Rosemary Curb argues convincingly that the nightmare in *A Lesson in Dead Language* takes place in a "Catholic school" and that the White Dog's mask concealing a blank face and the costume looking "great, stiff, [and] white" suggests the habit of a nun.[22] As the official language of the Church for two millennia, Latin is the cornerstone of Christianity and has historically been used in the Mass, Scripture, edicts, encyclicals, and decrees. Both sexually and theologically appropriate, then, Latin is a dead language in Kennedy's play. The seven pupils' innocence has expired just as the Latin they will be forced to learn, speak, and write. Their Latin lessons represent the death of childhood happiness.

Latin has other symbolic values in *A Lesson in Dead Language*. Though the language may have been moribund in the 1960s when Kennedy wrote *A Lesson in Dead Language,* the vestiges of its rule are still lethal, as the girls find out. It is the language of white power—precisely the point of the lesson in the classics that the draconian White Dog impresses on these seven black pupils. Undeniably, the White Dog, like those who taught in parochial schools, becomes the guardian of a classical tradition of Latin instruction and power. As the gatekeeper of this white educational system, the White Dog represents the discipline and punishment such a school, steeped in Greco-Roman culture, inflicts on the seven black girls. Though they are being taught about the language enshrining a white ideology, the girls are prohibited from enjoying its cultural heritage. A white culture forces them to repeat its learning but prevents them from possessing it. The White Dog's last words, "Translate what I read" (46), both control what the girls can and should do in their lives and censor their feelings, thoughts, and even their nightmares.

Kennedy's additional use of Roman Catholic symbols and rituals occurs in and through the crèche figures of Joseph, Mary, Jesus, two Wise Man, and a shepherd, who become agents of punishment in the girls' tragedy, as they were even more menacingly in *A Rat's Mass*. First seen as venerated figures, the Holy Family "were friends of my childhood" (46), admits one of the pupils, reinforcing the girls' perceived earlier acceptance by a white-dominated culture and religion, as well as the hope of security therein. But as these young black girls mature into women, the classically rooted white church, in their unconscious, abhors and abandons them. In the chain of Kennedy's psychic plot, the crèche characters are transformed into "*statues of Romans*" (46), symbolizing the dead classical world coming to life to harass and endanger the fertile black girls. Rather than representing the sacred mysteries of human birth and divine love, these religious figures in *A Lesson in Dead Language* stand for the oppressive world of the sterile intellect of Rome, antithetical to free, unspoiled black femininity. Again, a "white ratiocinative culture kills."[23] As in *A Rat's Mass* and *The Owl Answers*, sacred things are desecrated to theatricalize the horrors of the girls' sexual initiation.

The lemon figures in Roman Catholic symbolism as well. "The lemon is a symbol of fidelity in love, and as such, is often associated with the Virgin Mary."[24] This fruit thus forges an ironic link between the innocent black girls and the Virgin, represented by the statue and reinforced in one pupil's refrain: "I am bleeding, Mother" (45). Not unintentionally, Kennedy here ironically evokes Mary as the traditional patron of mothers. In another instance of ritualistic associations with the Virgin and with childhood innocence, *June and Jean in Concert*'s Jean, representing Kennedy, is dressed like the Virgin Mary. But such holy connections in *A Lesson in Dead Language* dissolve when the girls reach menses and are spurned by the crèche Virgin. The lemon symbolism extends to another crèche figure, Saint Joseph, as well. Anna Chupa describes the rituals of the Saint Joseph's Day altars, which lend insight to Kennedy's play: "It was good luck to steal a lemon from the altar leaving hidden coins behind for the poor . . . a lemon blessed on St. Joseph's altar will not turn black and is a symbol of good luck. Lemons are for young married women who want to become pregnant."[25] In this religious context, the girls' votive intentions are thwarted when they can no longer play a game of lemons and, consequently, must forfeit the happiness and blessings such fruit promises. Losing their lemons consigns the girls to a hopeless, sinful world. Having grown up in a neighborhood with a large Italian population, Kennedy would have known about the Saint Joseph altar.

Perhaps the most significant physical symbols in the play, again merging religious and sexual themes, are the girls' white organdy dresses, each of which has *"a great circle of blood on the back"* (44).[26] Both the color white and the blood, in Kennedy's associative chain of psychic experiences, have numerous, overlapping meanings. On one level, blood represents menses, the girls' entering the world of womanhood and childbearing that a condemning white world stigmatizes. But the white organdy uniforms can alternatively suggest First Communion dresses and veils, apparel that metaphorically refers to the hymeneal veil, which, when broken, bleeds just as the girls' dresses do.[27] The color white in this context may theologically stand for the girls' sexually innocent bodies before penetration. But it can also suggest the opposite. Blood on their dresses is not a sacramental sign, but can represent sullied purity, a badge of shame emblazoned on them in the White Dog's classroom. To a prejudiced society that ostracizes black pupils, the color white enshrines a purity to which they are not entitled. Though dressed in white, they cannot pass for white just as Sarah in *Funnyhouse of a Negro* could not, despite her shrine enthroning white objects.[28]

It is worth emphasizing, too, that their white dresses streaked with blood may allude to the well-known paradox from the book of Revelation (7:14–15)—"The redeemed wash their white robes in the blood of the Lamb"—foreshadowing their martyrdom and spiritual/communal cleansing into sainthood. In *A Lesson in Dead Language*, however, this ritualistic sign of salvation is perversely twisted by a cruel white society, where whiteness is further associated with killing. Recall that the vengeful Rosemary in *A Rat's Mass* wears a white Communion dress. In Kennedy's terrifying mythology, then, these young girls have washed their robes not in the blood of the Lamb but in the condemnation of the White Dog, bringing them guilt, not salvation. They must stand with their backs to the audience as misbehaving pupils do in a corner of a classroom for punishment and humiliation. In *A Lesson in Dead Language*, these black girls enter the world of the apocalypse.

CHAPTER 5

Acting White

A Movie Star Has to Star in Black and White

After *Funnyhouse of a Negro*, *A Movie Star Has to Star in Black and White* may be Kennedy's most well-known play. It premiered in a workshop production in November 1976 at the New York Public Theater and was "recovered" at the Signature Theatre in 1995 in a season dedicated to Kennedy's plays.[1] Both productions were directed by Joseph Chaikin, artistic director of the Signature and Kennedy's longtime friend. With *Movie Star*, Kennedy turns to another icon of white society—the cinema—to show how this cultural medium expresses the fears and fantasies of a black woman tormented by a legacy of prejudice. Kennedy painfully unravels the tragic incongruity of such fantasies "in a prose-poem of black birthright and tragedy."[2] She creates a character, again named Clara, to speak through and in dialogue with female movie stars from three blockbuster romantic films from the 1940s and 1950s—*Now, Voyager* (1942), *Viva Zapata!* (1952), and *A Place in the Sun* (1951). But these stars do not speak lines from their respective films, nor do they go by the names of the characters whom they played. In fact, Kennedy uses no lines from these films. Rather, in their own names, the stars narrate Clara's memories of her suffering with her husband, Eddie, and of her parents, who recoiled from segregation and experienced a rancorous divorce.

The immediate context for *A Movie Star*, though, is Clara's coming home in October 1963 to visit her brother in the hospital after he had been injured in an automobile accident that left him "brain damaged and paralyzed" (77). Members of Clara's family join her and the stars in Kennedy's metadrama using period costumes, movie music (including the passionate score from *Now, Voyager*), shadows, lighting, and multiple sets. Reviewing the 1995 production, David Willinger provocatively remarked, "*Movie Star* evokes the uncanny atmosphere of black and white films—cool, chatty and redolent with both anxiety and glamour. The glamour is ironic, since it violates the apparent banality of Clara's midwestern family's life."[3]

Blending these different worlds, *Movie Star* appropriately opens with a prologue spoken by the Columbia Pictures Lady, a character representing the white woman in a long silver dress standing on a pedestal and holding a torch seen at the beginning of numerous Columbia films. Framing the action, this Columbia Pictures Lady also ends *Movie Star,* where audiences see a "*brief dazzling image*" of her. The white color of this film icon and the advertised mission of Columbia Pictures—"to bring light to the world"—allow Kennedy from the start to the finish of *Movie Star* to play, visually and verbally, on the light and dark imagery found in her other works. Symbolically, therefore, Kennedy emphasizes that "*all the colors* [in *Movie Star*] *are shades of black and white*" (62). Functioning as the chorus, the Columbia Pictures Lady explains the crucial casting system in Kennedy's play: "The leading roles are played by Bette Davis, Paul Henreid, Jean Peters, Marlon Brando, Montgomery Clift and Shelley Winters. Supporting roles are played by the mother, the father, the husband. A bit role is played by Clara" (63). The script stresses that the actors playing the stars "*all look exactly like their movie roles*" (63). *Movie Star* is thus saturated with the film lore of these three classics.

The world of film is an appropriate cultural site for Kennedy's continuing investigation into how a black woman exists in a white society that casts her in a subordinate role. Like the heroines in *Funnyhouse of a Negro, The Owl Answers, A Lesson in Dead Language,* and *A Rat's Mass,* Clara in *Movie Star* grapples with questions of identity—who am I, who do I speak for, what do people see when they see me, who do they say I am, and am I black or white? And like Sarah in *Funnyhouse of a Negro* and Clara in *The Owl Answers,* this Clara is a splintered, fragmented self. Her various selves are projected through the three stars—Bette Davis, Jean Peters, and Shelley Winters—as well as through her own character. She assumes multiple roles, physicalized and represented through the stars that speak for her, to her parents, to her husband, or about her self. "Clara has become a living voice over."[4] But, ironically, Clara is estranged from the very self she is creating in *Movie Star.* Seeing her write in her diaries, Clara's husband Eddie accuses her of being "a spectator watching [her] life like watching a black and white movie" (75). As one critic argued, "The tragic heroine, Clara, watches her bit-part life like a spectator at black-and-white movies, except that her voice possesses those of the white movie-star icons."[5] Spectatorship does not ensure freedom, but links Clara to "cinematic images manipulated by a specific technology" that reduces women to racist and sexist roles.[6] Using film techniques again, Kennedy explores a character's emotional states in a struggle against racism. Self-representation becomes a process of imitation for Clara, as it did for Sarah.

Clara's troubled negotiations with self and others are charted through her relationship to the stars. They are her narrative voices. A key stage direction reads, "*Instead of Clara,*

Bette Davis replies" (68). Davis voices Clara's fears about her husband: "I get very jealous of you, Eddie. You're doing something with your life" (68). When Clara worries about her father, Davis, again as a projection of Clara, speaks, "My father tried to commit suicide once when I was in high school" (69). A little later, Jean Peters talks for and stars as Clara, expressing a memory filled with pain. "This reminds me of when Eddie was in Korea and I had the miscarriage" (73). The third star, Shelley Winters, exteriorizes still another part of Clara's fractured self when she recalls Clara's father's feelings after he divorced her mother: "This morning [he] came by again. . . . I want you to know my side. Now, your mother has always thought she was better than me" (76). Further blending Clara's life with these cinematic spokespersons for her thoughts, members of her family speak to the stars as if they were addressing her. These movie stars provide "the outer screen image" but it is really Clara's psyche that audiences hear.[7]

As in film, Kennedy juxtaposes these contrasting worlds on two different levels of representation. Clara's troubled life of family and marital problems, racial prejudice, and fear of miscarriage are set against, in, and through scenes from the three films starring these screen idols. This juxtaposition of black family members and white stars simultaneously maintains and subverts the fantasy of these imaginary dialogues.[8] We hear Clara's thoughts and ideas through Winters's dialogue, and we also see the movie star and the black woman side by side when "*Clara sits behind Shelley Winters*" in a "*small dark boat*" (74) in a scene from *A Place in the Sun*. Identities in this Kennedy play, as in her others, leak into, melt into, merge with, collide with, and assault one another. We are constantly asked to shift our views of identity—who, where, why, how, when.

These stars visually underscore the leading psychic issue for Clara and, in fact, for almost all of Kennedy's heroines—"Each day I wonder with what or with whom can I co-exist in a true union" (64). Apropos of her own career in the theater, Kennedy has stressed: "I always dreamed of being a great writer. A lot of my work comes from a dark inability to see where I fit in American society."[9] Failing with her family, her husband, and even herself, Clara is scattered across the roles of three of Hollywood's leading white stars. She tries to escape but realizes she can coexist only by seeing herself through a series of (re)presentations of actual stars playing parts in her life. But representation is not reality. Becoming is not the same as being. Reading Kennedy in light of Freudian views of identity ("self-sameness") and identification ("projecting the self onto another"), Elin Diamond concludes, "In *Movie Star,* more than in any other Kennedy text, the . . . [overlapping] of identification and identity becomes full-scale collision."[10]

The medium in which Clara inscribes herself ironically projects a powerfully negative social message about black women in a white world. A bastion and reflection of white taste and privilege, Hollywood has set the standards for beauty, love, glamour, success, and fandom.[11] In such a world, these virtues were the exclusive domain of white actors in films of the 1940s and 1950s, the time period of Clara's memory play. In *June and Jean in Concert* (1995), June exults in describing Ingrid Bergman, whose racial features she admires. Keeping "stacks of *Modern Screen*" in her vanity drawer, June makes "a scrapbook of my favorite pictures. I especially like pictures of people at parties in evening dress. And I keep another scrapbook on Ingrid Bergman. How marvelous to have a Swedish accent and a radiant smile" (248). Films validated and enforced these exclusive codes of white glamour society for a mass-culture audience.

Black women like Clara were inevitably marginalized, over-shadowed by white stars in films such as *Now, Voyager* or *A Place in the Sun.* With the exception of Lena Horne, whom Kennedy idolized in *People,* white Hollywood foreclosed on the chances of a black woman being a star in the 1940s and 1950s. Blacks were consigned to minor roles such as chauffeurs, maids, mammies, porters, janitors, and cooks.[12] Adhering to this Holly-wood policy in her own play, Clara casts herself—as stated by the Columbia Pictures Lady—in a "bit role," reinforcing the legacy of racial discrimination and typecasting. The privilege of being white thus perpetuated racial differences and identities, defining beauty and grace according to white-centered codes and distinctions. This cultural fiat explains one meaning behind the title of Kennedy's play: a movie star had to be white to star in the black and white films of these decades. Ironically, the racial connotations of black and white crucial to Kennedy's play have been mutated to cover sexual transgressions, as in the 2002 documentary film by Fenton Bailey and Randy Barbato, *Monica in Black and White,* about President Bill Clinton's (in)famous intern.[13]

But the title of Kennedy's play also suggests a radical, alter-native interpretation. Through Kennedy's transformative drama, a black woman, Clara, enters the white world of the "sanitized spectacle" of romance,[14] recasting her selves through such prominent actors as Bette Davis, Jean Peters, and Shelley Winters. Thus adjusted, Kennedy's title can be read as suggest-ing that a movie star has to star in a black woman's life/script just as she has to do in representing a white woman's life. Hav-ing these stars speak her thoughts, Clara is given a voice that potentially empowers her to star as a woman, a mother, a wife, and, eventually, a writer. She moves from being a bit player to center stage; she is on camera, not off. Her culturally forced silence and her marginalized role in American society can change when box office stars like Bette Davis and Shelley Winters speak Clara's thoughts.

Yet these stars attract the attention and applause that Clara's life never would. As Deborah Geis observes, "To inhabit a world of cinematic representation is to seek pleasure of transforming one's experiences into the experience of the idealized subject."[15] Transformed from a subordinate to the subject, Clara speaks the unspeakable in Hollywood. Her struggles and failures—as well as those of her family—acquire a Hollywood-like glamour and intensity. "Percolated through these quasi-mythic layers of Hollywood stars and scenarios, Clara's heartbreakingly mundane stories . . . assume a strange, shoddy grandeur."[16] In performing the roles of this black woman, the stars are recast, too, as members of a black family, acting out its sorrows and failures through their repertoire of selves. As a result, Kennedy subversively dismantles the principles of identity at the foundation of dominant white culture. As E. Bransley Brown intriguingly notes, by having white stars play a black woman, Kennedy turns the tables on the agency and image of colonialism.[17] She thus trumps "cinematic colonization,"[18] which, like colonial subjugation, required blacks and other marginalized groups to accept and be stereotyped by Hollywood's white casting system. Now it is time for the white world to imitate a black one.

But, tragically, these self-representations are neither healing nor self-fulfilling for Clara. She cannot escape the black identity that white society has imposed on her, as Kennedy shows through repeated and jarring contrasts between visual signs and verbal texts.[19] Even in her fantasy world, Clara is doomed. According to Geis again, the movie stars are ultimately a "reminder of her Otherness."[20] Clara might imagine them starring in and through her life, but these idols live in a Hollywood world that staunchly upholds the values of a white audience. A movie star is white even though she appears in a black and white medium. Reinforcing the point, the actors playing the stars "*look exactly like their movie roles*"; they are not black actors with white faces, as in *Funnyhouse of a Negro*. Bette Davis may speak for Clara, but she does not signify her in the world of Hollywood reality. She looks just like Bette Davis. Or, as Diamond points out, "it was . . . unacceptable . . . in the cultural discourses . . . that [Bette Davis] could represent" Kennedy, or Clara for that matter.[21] True to a consistent theme, Kennedy emphasizes the instability of her heroines' world of cruel memories/dreams/nightmares. Her plays embody this raging conflict between believing and seeing. In *June and Jean in Concert,* Kennedy later equated her grandmother's arrangement of family photos "with watching a film" at "the Waldorf on a Saturday afternoon" (252).

From the start, *Movie Star* signals through filmic techniques the clash of the black world of harsh reality and the white world of romantic fantasy. Like a filmmaker of her psyche, Clara employs flashbacks, close-ups, splices, cuts, and dissolves, often reminiscent of film noir, to link her life to that of the stars in *Now, Voyager, Viva Zapata!,* or *A Place in the Sun.* But like a whirling postmodern film, *Movie Star* forces audiences to shift and navigate through fluctuating identities and roles, time frames, locations, and perspectives repeatedly, sometimes simultaneously. One scene carries the vestiges of another as if bits and pieces of Clara's memory tagged along. Each scene is primarily devoted to one of these three films, but thanks to Kennedy's roving psychic camera, audiences see a lot of spillage. Scenes with the movie stars are intercut with those of Clara's family.[22] Clara's memories of her parents, brother, and husband dissolve into her own scripts. Though staged in a theater, *Movie Star* may be as close to a film as anything Kennedy has written.

Cinematically and psychologically crucial are the multiple sets on which the stars act out scenes from Clara's life. As scene 1 opens, Clara is in the hospital lobby waiting to see her injured brother, Wally, and meets her father and mother. Kennedy's own brother Cornell, who died in 1972, was hospitalized for nine years after an automobile accident. Setting the stage for Clara's dreamscape to *Now, Voyager,* the scene fades out from the white hospital room and "*then bright lights . . . convey an ocean liner in motion*" (64). Clara as Bette Davis "*walks slowly*" on the deck with a silent Paul Henreid, the leading man, and the lobby is transformed into that famous scene from *Now, Voyager.* These multiple sets evoke the two worlds of Clara's life—the hospital and the world of her cinematic escape. Blending into one another, the sets both reinforce and clash with Clara's world of reality. The romantic cruise ship set is out of place in the cruel reality of the hospital lobby. Yet dividing and blocking the stage through lighting and sound between the hospital lobby and the fantasy cruise ship, Kennedy brilliantly visualizes the fragmentary and artificial world of Clara's ephemeral dream landscape.

Kennedy represents Clara's psychic journey through the dualities of characters as well as sets and times. Clara is not alone in her voyage. She is accompanied by and believes she is protected through Bette Davis, with whom she imaginatively professes she has something in common. In *Now, Voyager,* Bette Davis plays Charlotte Vale, who is (re)cast from a dowdy spinster into an attractive woman who meets the suave but unhappily married Paul Henreid character on the ship. Joining Bette Davis, Clara is on a similar voyage that she dreams might transform her into a successful, fulfilled woman. In her imaginative play/film, Clara is both black woman and white movie star simultaneously. Through this stardom, Clara takes audiences on a voyage back in time, splicing events from the film with those of her life and her parents'. As the scene begins, it is June of 1955, a crucial time in Clara's marriage to Eddie. Familiar Kennedy imagery conveys that she is terrified of what will happen when her baby is born: "I wonder will I turn into a river of blood and die" (64). Speaking through Bette Davis, Clara panics that Eddie will not be there "except for his photo" and later exclaims, "All that bleeding. I'll never forgive him" (67).

Clara also uses Bette Davis, as both actor and character in *Now, Voyager,* to uncover wounds that run generations deep in her own family. Juxtaposing black characters and white star in this opening scene underscores Clara's precarious and fragmented identity. Through a nonlinear plot, Kennedy elides time to 1929 and earlier still to express her mother's and father's nightmares, while Clara is simultaneously in 1963 reflecting on the traumas of 1955. Clara's parents were victims of Jim Crow laws as well as cruelty toward each other, resulting in mutual recrimination. Her mother blames her father for leaving her to marry a "girl who talks to willow trees," and her father, who wants to kill himself, takes audiences even further back in time in his desire to see his "mother and papa." Just as Clara cannot forgive Eddie for being absent, Clara's mother cannot forgive her father for his dereliction. Clara's pain is ensconced in her mother's. And her romantic dreams prove just as self-deceptive and hollow as her mother's. Her parents' hope of escaping prejudice by moving up north is doomed as much as Clara's believing in her romance with Eddie.

Kennedy plays upon differences between Clara's life and Bette Davis's role in *Now, Voyager.* Bette Davis's character

Charlotte Vale, however, triumphantly escapes from a domineering mother who wants her to remain an old maid, subservient and unloved. In a contrasting family dynamic, Clara cannot escape from her mother's legacy of failure in love. In another contrast, Davis raises Henreid's young daughter, who reminds her of the frightened and neurotic child she once was. However, Davis and Henreid happily accept a marriageless but loving relationship, without physical intimacy, for the sake of "their" daughter. On the other hand, Clara's miscarriage (verbally) contrasts with the visual and contextual clues and prompts inherent in Davis's character, who joyfully "births" Paul Henreid's child without bloodletting. By showing Clara's family traumas in light of *Now, Voyager, Movie Star* resonates with additional irony and disappointments. The film plot becomes a subtext for events, seen and unseen, in Clara's life.

Carrying over the same cinematic techniques from scene 1, Kennedy evocatively transports audiences to *Viva Zapata!* in scene 2, where Clara continues her psychic odyssey. "*There is no real separation from hospital to Viva Zapata*" (70), thanks to the "*shadows and light*" (72) from the lobby to Wally's hospital room and the haunting transitions provided by "*movie music.*" Moving into the next scene and film set, Clara simply "*walks along the deck and into the door*" (69), leaving a loving Paul Henreid and Bette Davis at the ship's railing. "*She arrives at the hospital doorway, then enters her brother's room*" (69). Incorporating the visual details from *Now, Voyager* into the *Viva Zapata!* set, Kennedy claims that such movement is "*like a ship in motion*" (71), fusing the two movie sets. The silent but loving film couple of Davis and Henreid continues to contrast with Clara, who experiences even greater pain in scene 2—"Her brother is in a coma"—signaled by the arrival of a pair of new movie idols from *Viva Zapata!* Filmed in black and white in

1952, this Hollywood hit unrolls the rousing biography of Emiliano Zapata (played by Brando), a Mexican revolutionary who fought to free peasants from a tyrannical regime. He is loved by Josefa Espejo (Jean Peters) and his own tempestuous, loyal brother Eufemio (Anthony Quinn). In this highly romanticized film, celebrating the life, loves, and death of a cultural hero, the electrifying love scenes between Brando and Peters contrast with Clara's estrangement and divorce from Eddie.

On one level it is easy to separate the white movie star couple from Clara and her family. Visually (re)creating *Viva Zapata!*, the Brando and Peters characters of *Movie Starr* kiss tenderly on their wedding night as music plays and they are bathed in "*dazzling wedding light*," another reminder of the exclusivity of white actors in film, although, ironically, Brando and Peters wear dark makeup to resemble Mexicans. They then (re)enact the famous "teach me to read" scene as Peters intimately helps Brando to become a more powerful leader. Opposed to Jean Peters's loving instruction, Clara and her mother, through these recuperated movie stars, sadly read aloud a bitter script from their blighted relationships with the men they once loved. The poignant visual message from the film jars against Clara's verbalized memories of her marriage articulated through Peters. Caught between and in her dreams and the film, Clara recalls through Peters that "after I lost the baby . . . [I] decided I wanted to get a divorce when Eddie came back from Korea" (70). Yet it is Clara who, a little later, remembers that "Eddie looked at me with such sadness. It fills me with hatred for him and myself" (72). Weaving and blending identities through successive lines of dialogue, Peters declares, "my brother Wally's still alive," and in the next line it is Clara who talks "to her diary," recording "Wally was in an accident" (71).

As in scene 1 with *Now, Voyager,* Kennedy manipulates visual cues from *Viva Zapata!* in scene 2 to explore still deeper levels of hurt in Clara's life. In Clara's monologues spoken through Peters, movie star roles are (re)claimed and (re)apportioned to express events and views unique to Clara's life history. Appropriate for Clara's dream world sequences, beds become the controlling symbols in scene 2 as Kennedy circulates movie myths and Clara's psychic history around them. Peters sits on a bed with Brando, suggesting their wedded love, but when recalling Clara's miscarriage, Peters *"is bleeding [and] falls back on the bed. Brando pulls a sheet out from under her. The sheets are black"* (70). Emblematic of the scene as a whole, Brando *"continuously helps Jean Peters change sheets. He puts the black sheets on the floor around them."* This stage business, of course, recalls Clara's bloody miscarriage, leading to the death of her child and her marriage.

Additionally, Brando and Peters's *"continuously"* pulling the sheet off the bed may symbolize Clara's horror over the miscarriage and separation from Eddie. Accordingly, the black sheets—antithetical to being Hollywood symbols of sexual passion—can now reflect Clara's failed marriage, and her mother's as well. But, paradoxically, the black sheets may also signify the black lives/roles played by a white movie star, as Bette Davis did in scene 1. Finally, the bed on which Peters falls, covering the black sheets with blood, suggests as well Wally's hospital bed—for all practical purposes his living coffin—ominously present on stage. These harrowing Kennedyesque symbols—beds, black sheets, blood—present Clara's multiple selves through multiple identities and signifiers.

Through *Viva Zapata!,* Clara is also able to record her feelings about the men in her life, all of whom have been disconnected from her. On the one hand, the "heroic and tender" Zapata, as played by Brando and whose life and death mark the dignity of the man and the pride of those who loved him, is the (im)possible model for Eddie, Clara's father, and her brother Wally. Contrasting with Zapata, Eddie is unromantic, absent, ineffectual. Similarly, her father is weak and thin. He wears a funny shirt and straw hat cocked to one side, drinks, and is abusive toward her mother. He evokes pity more than he represents valor. Zapata's spirited relationship with his hard-fighting brother Eufemio is also very different from the relationship Clara has with Wally. In the recycled events of scene 3, she describes visiting Wally, when he was imprisoned in the army stockade; ignominiously, "his head was shaven and he didn't have on any shoes" (77). Even though Zapata was imprisoned by Mexican dictator Porfirio Díaz, he remained unconquered. Played by Brando, Zapata can be the hero in Clara's life the way her spouse, father, or brother cannot be.

In scene 3, the most ambitious and daring in *Movie Star*, Kennedy juggles three different sets of movie-star characters from the three films all on one stage. Using the resources of the stage to imitate those of film, she once more takes full advantage of lighting, movie music, props, costumes, and multiple sets. Within Wally's hospital room, which is symbolically "dark," the *"lights of the ship from Now, Voyager"* go on (74). Looking at photos of Clara's parents, Jean Peters from *Viva Zapata!* recalls the rooms in Clara's childhood house, especially Wally's old room, where he lived before the accident. As *"Jean Peters and Brando stare at each other. A small dark boat from [the] side opposite Wally's room"* appears with Montgomery Clift rowing Shelley Winters, with Clara sitting behind her (74), as Kennedy introduces the stars from the play's third film, *A Place in the Sun*

(1951). As "*Clift silently rows [the] dark boat across,*" Eddie talks to Jean Peters about Clara's desire to be a writer. After this short conversation, "*Clara from the boat*" in *Place in the Sun* (75) admits, as Kennedy herself did when she was denied acceptance as an English major at Ohio State, "Everyone says it's unrealistic for a Negro to want to write" (75). Eddie continues talking to Peters (as Clara) and, distraught over Clara's incessant reminders of how different they are, leaves the stage for good. In between, Shelley Winters speaks for Clara, reminiscing painfully about her parents and her father's "wanting her to know my side." Throughout, Clara talks to her diary, recites lines from her play *The Owl Answers,* and reads from her notebook. Kennedy skillfully mutes some characters as she pours words of deep pain into others, permitting us to see failed dreams in the dark. At least five different conversations go on in this scene—Eddie with Jean Peters, Eddie with Clara, Winters to Montgomery Clift, Shelley Winters and Clara sharing a speech about Wally's condition, and Peters communicating with Brando as they continue to change the sheets and "*stare at each other*" (96). The polyphony of voices and the shifting sets represent the frenzy inside Clara's psyche.

As with *Now, Voyager* and *Viva Zapata!,* Kennedy asks audiences to recall key settings and characters from *A Place in the Sun* to grasp parallels between this film and Clara's life and dreams. Based on Theodore Dreiser's 1931 novel, *An American Tragedy, A Place in the Sun* chronicles another frustrated, doomed love affair, which has grave implications for Clara's relationship with Eddie and serves as inspiration for her future as a writer. Telling the story of a love triangle, *A Place in the Sun* stars Montgomery Clift as George Easton, who briefly dates Shelley Winters's Alice Tripp and whom he gets pregnant. But then he falls in love with and intends to marry the wealthy

Angela Vickers, played by Elizabeth Taylor. When Shelley Winters threatens to blackmail Clift, ruining his chances for social advancement if he does not marry her, Clift takes her out in a rowboat to drown her. But he cannot go through with the plan and, in an ironic twist, Winters drowns nevertheless. Faithful to the film, *Movie Star* ends "*Quite suddenly, as Shelley Winters stands up and falls 'into the water.' She is in the water, only her head is visible, calling silently. Montgomery Clift stares at her*" as she calls silently (77). Finally, "*Shelley Winters drowns. Light goes down on Montgomery Clift as he stares at Shelley Winters drowning*" (78), an ironic inversion of Clara's spectatorship of her life through films.

Kennedy takes audiences full circle from a romantic cruise ship in *Now, Voyager* to a tragic rowboat in *Place in the Sun*. But, above all, Shelley Winters's tragedy elucidates Clara's in many ways. Questing like Winters's character Alice, Clara wants her place in the sun as well. But Eddie leaves Clara just as Clift did Winters. In yet another parallel, Winters loses her baby in the film just as Clara did through miscarriage. As a powerful but subtextual parallel to Winters's drowning, Clara nearly tumbles to her death when holding her mother in the hospital after Wally's injury. Mother "shook so I thought both of us were going to fall headlong down the steps" (78). Moreover, just as no one hears or responds to Winters's call, Clara, too, feels that her family and husband do not respond to her as a writer. Winters's drowning, silent voice is a perfect *tableau mordant* for a Kennedy heroine who views herself as a writer. Like Shelley Winters, Clara drowns, amid a sea of voices—her own, her family's, and the movie stars.

Not surprisingly, one of the most important themes in *Movie Star*, as in *The Owl Answers*, is the act of writing itself— the process by which Clara's (and Kennedy's) memories are recorded. Marc Robinson ingeniously argues that the title of Kennedy's play refers to the very act of writing: "The black and white of the title is really the black ink on the white typing paper."[23] Beyond doubt, Kennedy inscribes herself in Clara's dedication to her craft of writing. Clara's fictive and Kennedy's real "selves overlap. Clara is Kennedy's surrogate and, like Kennedy, she is writing her wounds."[24] At times, we hear in Clara's voice a timid and apprehensive Adrienne Kennedy, unsure of her early work when she submitted and then wanted to withdraw *Funnyhouse of a Negro* from Edward Albee's workshop. Clara "aspires to be a writer but she cannot imagine a black voice in the white world she lives in."[25] As Kennedy did, Clara creates her plays through personal narratives recorded in diaries and scrapbooks. Talking for Clara, who is really talking for Kennedy, Bette Davis confesses: "In the scrapbook that my father left is a picture of my mother in Savannah, Georgia in 1921." Just as Kennedy won an Obie for *Funnyhouse of a Negro* in 1964, Clara informs her mother, "I've just won an award and I'm going to have a play produced" (71).

Ultimately, Clara in *Movie Star* allows Kennedy to revoice the fears she felt about her career on the verge of its beginning in 1963. Clara, like Kennedy, notates her work with comparisons between bloody bodies and scripts. Kennedy thus "establishes [a connection] between bleeding and artistic creation."[26] As E. Barnsley Brown stresses, Kennedy "creates a narrative in which she is simultaneously both present and absent, both represented and (re)presented,"[27] thanks to Clara and her movie stars. Yet, according to Marc Robinson, *Movie Star* ends on a very positive note that expresses Kennedy's victorious survival: "By writing an image of herself writing, Kennedy . . . insists on the permanence and hard reality of her own vocation—the only stable aspect of a continuously mutating play."[28] Unlike Sarah, Clara from *The Owl Answers,* or Sister Rat in *A Rat's Mass,* this Clara, like Kennedy, is alive at the end to create the works that she has inscribed in *Movie Star.* It is Shelley Winters who drowns.

CHAPTER 6

The Alexander Plays

She Talks to Beethoven, The Ohio State Murders,
The Film Club, and Dramatic Circle

The Alexander Plays, published in 1992, contains the quartet *She Talks to Beethoven, The Ohio State Murders, The Film Club,* and *Dramatic Circle.* The collection was named for Suzanne Alexander, the protagonist in each play and a complex persona for Kennedy. Suzanne is a fictive prominent black dramatist whose works document the history of violence and prejudice against blacks. In presenting Suzanne at different times of her life and in different countries and conflicts, Kennedy mirrors many of her own traumas. Like Kennedy, Suzanne is an alumna of a prejudiced Ohio State University. In *She Talks to Beethoven,* Suzanne waits for her husband in Ghana, as Kennedy did for hers. In *The Film Club* and *Dramatic Circle,* set in London, Kennedy sketches a fictionalized portrait of the playwright and her family in 1961. Continuing Kennedy's earlier work, the Alexander plays are highly confessional.

These plays, however, mark a new phase in Kennedy's career in their diversity and their relationship to one another. Indebted to opera, *She Talks to Beethoven* is Kennedy's most optimistic play (excluding her adaptations *Lancashire Lad* and *The Lennon Play*). *The Ohio State Murders* is a psychic autobiography where an older Suzanne recalls and dramatizes, through a series of flashbacks, the hate crimes directed at her younger self. *The Film Club* is a monologue, and *Dramatic Circle* is a radio play. In all of these works, time and space are reconfigured through Suzanne's memory. There is no separation of past and present, only the struggle of a creative black woman playwright who shockingly replays and then fast-forwards her traumatized life. Yet the unifying theme of the Alexander plays is the triumph of art, music, and love over violence and prejudice.

She Talks to Beethoven

The first of the Alexander plays, *She Talks to Beethoven* is a distinctive script in Kennedy's canon. Unlike her earlier plays, it offers healing consolation instead of nightmarish terror. This play looks forward to happy conjugal and racial reconciliation. According to Lois More Overbeck, *She Talks to Beethoven* "discovers connections that comfort."[1] Set in "*Accra, Ghana, in 1961, soon after independence*" (139), the play relays the separation of Suzanne Alexander from her physician/artist husband, David. Previous to his being kidnapped or driven into hiding to protect his sick wife, David had been by Suzanne's bedside awaiting "the results of [her] undisclosed surgery" (143). While there, he "made sketches of his wife's illness and explained the progress and procedures to her" (143). The source of Suzanne's illness is undisclosed in Kennedy's sparse plot, and the circumstances of her husband's disappearance also remain cloudy. A supporter of the revolutionary poet Frantz Fanon (whose work he reads on a radio that periodically interrupts the play's dialogue), David "was hated for his writing on the clinics and Fanon, and for his statements on the mental condition of the colonized patients" (143). Suzanne spends much of her time looking for David to return and talking with Beethoven. The play is an extended conversation between Beethoven (1770–1827) and Suzanne (30 years old at the time) as they freely and warmly talk and travel with each other. Places, gender, and race merge through parallels between the black woman writer and the white male composer.

Kennedy uses anachronisms and geography to challenge racial stereotypes and identities.[2] Beethoven visits Suzanne's Africa as she does his Vienna, and vice versa. She accompanies him as he accompanies her. Beethoven is made flesh in Suzanne's Ghana. In Accra, Beethoven lives in the same delightful white stucco house from which his music emanates "among the fragrant flowers on the campus at Legon" (141). When she asks him if "your summers in Vienna" are unpleasantly hot, Beethoven responds, "Yes, like tonight here in Accra it was not pleasant . . . over a thousand horse-drawn cabs . . . raised a terrible dust . . . It was like a dirty fog" (142). In Accra, Beethoven consoles her: "I feel David will return by morning, perhaps on the road with the musicians, perhaps even in disguise" (145). Reciprocally, Suzanne asks the great composer, "may I visit you next spring" (147) in Vienna, and psychically and physically, she accompanies Beethoven to see his nephew there: "We could still walk to Karl's house near the Danube and look into his window. Perhaps you can call to him" (144). After this visit, Beethoven cautions, "We won't get back to Dobling until nearly four now" (144). Suzanne is in Vienna when Beethoven dies.

Vienna and Accra are also linked as cities under siege, yet the violence in Beethoven's Vienna or Suzanne's Accra is not represented with graphic horror as in Kennedy's earlier plays. It is only related through dialogue. Accra is bathed in a climate of suspicion, plots, kidnappings. Suzanne stresses that both she and Beethoven are caught in *"the pale light of prisons"* (146). In *Dramatic Circle,* the play that follows *She Talks to Beethoven,* we hear about the tortures such prisoners suffer in Ghana. In embattled Vienna, Suzanne reads from one of Beethoven's published diaries: "the war with Napoleon escalated . . . Vienna is in great danger of being swept over by marauding Chasseurs" (140). Later, before the premiere of Beethoven's opera *Fidelio,* we hear that "To make matters worse, [Beethoven's] lodging was next to the city wall, and as Napoleon had ordered its destruction, blasts had just been set off under his windows" (143).

But in *She Talks to Beethoven* Kennedy does not dwell on the violence surrounding the composer's Vienna; rather she testifies to the influence his music had on her life and art. Throughout the play, Kennedy draws upon her own pleasant memories of musicians, especially Beethoven. Alisa Solomon aptly claims that "the action" of *She Talks to Beethoven* is "made up of . . . the process of turning memory into meaning."[3] In *People,* composers Robert Schumann, Claude Debussy, Frédéric Chopin, Giuseppe Verdi, and Richard Wagner coexist in the same world for Kennedy as do the spirituals, jazz ensembles, and compositions of Billy Eckstine, Nat King Cole, Judy Garland, Billie Holiday, and Duke Ellington. There is no valorizing of white or black music or musicians. All of these musical references contributed to Kennedy's memories of living in a world of experimentation, learning, and celebration. Nowhere is this more clearly articulated than in Kennedy's recollections in *People* of her piano teacher, Miss Eichenbaum. "The top of [Miss Eichenbaum's] piano was filled with photographs of her family and statues of Mozart, Beethoven and Chopin. At the end each year, at the time of the recital, she gave me another bust of a composer. It was because of Miss Eichenbaum I went to see the movie *A Song to Remember,* the story of Chopin's life" (*People,* 42). Encounters like these between white music teacher/mentor and black student were filed away in Kennedy's rolodex of memories.

In introducing Beethoven's works, Miss Eichenbaum encouraged the young Kennedy to incorporate art into a family context. Seeing the Eichenbaum family photos next to the bust of Beethoven reinforced the connection between the great composer and members of Kennedy's own family. Later, when she was a wife and a mother, Kennedy noted that she bought "a foot-high ivory statue" of Beethoven "at Pellenberg's on Broadway and put it on my desk for inspiration and read and reread Sullivan's books on the life of Beethoven—his spiritual development, his music . . . his growing deafness" (108). The seeds of love for classical music (Beethoven's, in particular) that Miss Eichenbaum planted in the young Adrienne Kennedy grew into her own choral composition—*She Talks to Beethoven.* No other composer in *People* receives more attention or earns fonder praise. Kennedy recalls that in 1956, when she was twenty-five years old, "I ordered all his string quartets from a record club. Each record was wrapped in delicate paper and the record covers were in romantic pale covers. How I treasured them" (86). As again she recalls in *People,* those string quartets "taught me that dark, impossible, unbearable moods could be transposed into work. A creative person could capture what he felt in andante, allegro, and molta bella" (87). These moods prompted her to create works that were, like Beethoven's, evocatively dark and mysteriously creative. In *She Talks to Beethoven,* the composer is seen in regard to her own African heritage and culture. Kennedy recalls, "I'd often stare at the statue of Beethoven I kept on the left-hand side of my desk. I felt it contained a 'secret.' I'd do the same with the photograph of Queen Hatshepsut that was on the wall. I did *not* then understand that I felt torn between these forces of my ancestry . . . European and African . . . a fact that would explode one day in my work" (96).

We see part of this ancestral clash emerge in *She Talks to Beethoven*. By recalling and conversing with Beethoven, Suzanne clarifies the family context of Kennedy's experience at school and later in life that associated musicians with family. As members of the same creative family, Beethoven and Suzanne will break all of the color, time, and gender barriers that fragment, categorize, or valorize art. The famed composer becomes Suzanne's other self, or confidant, a role often supplied by another woman such as the twins in *June and Jean in Concert* or her younger self in *The Ohio State Murders*. The dialogue in *She Talks to Beethoven* both acknowledges and incorporates a black diaspora honoring the work of the Alexanders, David and Suzanne, as talented black artists. As the play evolves, Suzanne's relationship with Beethoven demonstrates that artists can transcend the dichotomies of white or black, male or female. Queen Hatshepsut and Beethoven—black and white, woman and man, African and European—can coexist profitably in Kennedy's memory and art. Artistically and memorially, black Africa and white Vienna become the same location; Beethoven and Hatshepsut are parents of the same artistic development that led to Kennedy's work. In *She Talks to Beethoven*, Kennedy does not feel torn between her two heritages.

Accordingly, Kennedy symbolically links Suzanne and Beethoven throughout the play, especially in their sickness, pain, and even their physicality, continuing to erase conflicting categories of race and gender. The wild hair associated with

Kennedy's black protagonists is transferred to the white composer. "The neglect of his person which he exhibited gave him a somewhat wild appearance. His features were strong and prominent; his eye was full of rude energy; his hair, which neither comb nor scissors seemed to have visited for years, overshaded his broad brow in a quantity and confusion to which only the snakes round a Gorgon's head offer a parallel" (141). This description of Beethoven, with its emphasis on his gory and exaggerated hair, seems more appropriate to Sarah or Clara, the black protagonists of Kennedy's earlier plays. In the process, Kennedy reconfigures identities based on race and nationality through the shared symbolism of hair and attacks racist ideologies by physically linking Beethoven to these black women. Thus, Beethoven helps to express Suzanne (and Kennedy herself) as she helps to express him.

Like David and Suzanne, who are "an inseparable couple" (143), Suzanne and Beethoven read and generate their work in the same playing area, that is, in the same play. Hearing Beethoven's music and Suzanne's voice, audiences see both of them composing, scores and manuscripts, respectively (144). The two artists share secrets, lament maladies, and inscribe ideas in each other's works. Beethoven instructs Suzanne to write in his conversation books: "You must write what you want to say to me in them. I cannot hear you" (147). His diaries appear in *She Talks to Beethoven* and, reciprocally, David's messages to Suzanne are written in Beethoven's conversation books. "Ludwig, why is David's handwriting in your conversation books? This poem is in David's own handwriting" (147), Suzanne exclaims. Through the process of creation—the written word and the musical score—a familial bond is struck between a composer of music and a composer of musical words.

Beethoven is given renewed life through Suzanne's play just as she is given new life (hope, memory) through Ludwig's conversation books in which David, her collaborator, appropriates space for her benefit and even leaves poems for her between the pages of the composer's books.

Given this intimate relationship between Beethoven and Suzanne, then, it is fitting that the composer's last abode, and the last place the two visit, is "the Schwarzspanierhaus, the House of the Black Spaniard, to the west of the old city walls" (149). Though Beethoven dies "unconscious" and "broken," he does so nobly in a house associated with a black presence. Ethnographically and paradoxically, the "Black Spaniard" suggests yet again the blend of white and black races exhibited in the close relationship between Beethoven and Suzanne and in the way Kennedy connects white imagery with Suzanne's "delightful stucco house" in Legon where Beethoven plays. It may be bitterly cold, with white snow swirling around the Schwarzspanierhaus, portending death in the outside world as it does in *The Ohio State Murders,* but the interior of that house suggests, by its name, the union of Beethoven and Suzanne as kindred artists.[4]

Yet the most compelling connection between Suzanne and Beethoven surfaces in the relationship of Kennedy's play to Beethoven's celebrated opera, *Fidelio,* references to which become a vital element in *She Talks to Beethoven.* Paul K. Bryant-Jackson maintains that Kennedy "uses Beethoven's *Fidelio* (the transitional work to 'Romanticism') as the cantina of *She Talks* to underscore Suzanne's transcendental desire."[5] But the opera has an even greater structural importance. Through the numerous references to the opera in Kennedy's play, *Fidelio* encourages readers to make the same types of analogies that the film scripts in *Movie Star* offer or that Thomas Hardy's *Tess of the D'Urbervilles* does in *The Ohio State Murders*. Kennedy incorporates *Fidelio* as she translocates it, making Beethoven's opera present in her African experience and vice versa. Strains of *Fidelio* are heard in Legon. In Vienna and Accra, Beethoven talks about rehearsals and the problems he encounters with *Fidelio*. As *She Talks to Beethoven* begins, "the production of *Fidelio* was anticipated by months of increasing tension as the war with Napoleon escalated" (140); later we hear "*the orchestra rehearsing Fidelio*" (147); and, finally, we accompany Suzanne to the opening night performance, where Beethoven's "permanent infirmity" prevents him from hearing singers, orchestra, or applause. But, thanks to artistic memory and coalescing chronology, we hear Beethoven's opera with its most (auto)biographical amplification. For through Suzanne's memory, *Fidelio* is inscribed in *She Talks to Beethoven* as Suzanne's pain is inscribed through the ecstasy of Beethoven's opera.

Poignantly yet subtly, Kennedy draws upon Beethoven's opera to shape and conclude her own play optimistically. Like *Fidelio*, *She Talks to Beethoven* is a work of great faith in human love and freedom, symbolized through a couple's unalterable fidelity in the throes of adversity. In both works, a couple is separated because of political treachery, sending one of the spouses into bondage. In *Fidelio*, Florestan, a Spanish noble, is unjustly imprisoned in Seville, bereft of any hope of rescue. Similarly, David is driven away because of "threats against his life" and to protect Suzanne from danger. Both husbands have been banished into absence. The central concern of opera and play, though, is on the faithful wives who aid their husbands. Florestan's wife Leonore disguises herself as a young man, Fidelio, who works in the Seville prison. When Florestan is sentenced to death, Leonore/Fidelio intervenes, thwarts the execution, and frees her spouse from his chains. Analogously, Suzanne keeps David alive through her creative work, in which he remains a vital part. In effect, Suzanne unshackles David from the shadows of deathlike absence by bringing him into the forefront of her dialogue with Beethoven and into the opera *Fidelio*.

But Kennedy mirrors *Fidelio* even further by having David disguise himself to help Suzanne continue with her life and work. David's creative soul remains unharmed by being included in those Beethoven works that Suzanne consults and commends to us within her play. At the end of the play, for example, Suzanne addresses David, "You sent Beethoven until you returned. Didn't you?" And David's voice "(*Not unlike Beethoven's*)" responds, "I knew he would console you while I was absent" (150). Using the central device of Beethoven's opera (Leonore's disguise as Fidelio), Kennedy disguises David as Beethoven to keep him present, alive. In this climactic moment, *She Talks to Beethoven* powerfully emphasizes the bonds that exist between Beethoven and Suzanne. A black artist/husband and white composer share identities, becoming a collaborating team to communicate artistically, even intimately, with a black woman writer/wife.

The Film Club

Although *The Film Club* and *Dramatic Circle* follow *The Ohio State Murders* in *The Alexander Plays*, it is easier to understand their dramatic contexts if they are discussed immediately after *She Talks to Beethoven*. *The Film Club* continues the mystery of David Alexander's disappearance and the ways in which Suzanne comes to terms with her grief. The shortest of the

Alexander plays, *The Film Club* flows smoothly into the last play in the collection, *Dramatic Circle,* which elaborates on it. Set in London, *The Film Club* finds Suzanne recounting the "events of Winter 1961" as she awaits news about her kidnapped husband. Unable to remain in Accra because of her high-risk pregnancy, Suzanne is joined by David's sister, Alice, whose interest in film (like Kennedy's own) provides the title for the play. Adapting Hollywood classics such as *Now, Voyager,* which Kennedy featured in *Movie Star,* Alice "typed our scripts, directed, and filmed scenes with all of us playing parts" (174). Suzanne recalls, "I see her . . . arranging us all for the camera" (179). It is significant that *The Film Club* begins with Alice's summary of an earlier Bette Davis film where one twin sister "pretends to be her twin" to "gain" a man's love. With its emphasis on mistaken, transferred, and stolen identities, this film sets the stage for what follows. Suzanne creates her own film club as she adapts and assigns herself roles from a variety of scripts to represent events that are "*so strange / and uncanny*" (179).

Subtitled "*A Monologue,*" *The Film Club* is a polyphony of voices from inscribed texts, a proven Kennedy dramatic strategy. Suzanne encircles audiences in a web of texts—films, stories, letters, reports, poems, medical diagnoses, and nightmares. Within the frame of Alice's film club, Suzanne takes us into her doctor's therapy sessions. Dr. Freudenberger (a Kennedyesque Freud) includes Alice and Suzanne "in a theatrical reading he was working on with patients" (175). Like Alice, who adapts scripts and inserts family members in them, Dr. Freudenberger asks Alice and Suzanne to read lines from Bram Stoker's *Dracula,* the ultimate horror story of kidnapping, lost/stolen identities, and nightmares. Ironically, he assigns Suzanne the part of Lucy, one of Dracula's victims who "sleepwalks," has her blood consumed, and is later given "a blood transfusion," but is taken again by Dracula after a wolf breaks her window. At last, "Lucy dies" (177). Suzanne vicariously acquires Lucy's terror. "Strongly . . . affected by the passages I read on Lucy," Suzanne "began to utter them in my sleep" (176). Stoker's wolf joins Kennedy's menacing menagerie of owls, white dogs, rats, jackals, and bats. Later, in an attack on colonialism, Suzanne recites a horrific poem by David Diop (1927–1960), a West African poet who opposed French colonialism. Diop's "Vultures" is about Dracula-like predatory beasts, who with their claws *were setting up / the bloody monument of the / guardian era* (177). Reinforcing the haunting effect of Stoker's script on her, Suzanne reads a passage about Jonathan Harker, another Dracula victim, who discovers his "personal effects [are] gone," is forced to "write . . . misleading letters to England," and learns that Dracula dressed in his clothes stole a child for "three vampire women" (178). The child's "bereft mother is [then] killed by wolves."

Like Lucy and Harker, Suzanne becomes a victim of *"terror encompassed . . . on every side"* (176). In Freudenberger's sessions, her own identity and psychic peace are under scrutiny. She exhibits Lucy's symptoms. "David's family said I lapsed into sleeplessness, hysteria." Moreover, like Lucy "on the East cliff," Suzanne is "found . . . wandering along the Embankment near More's Gardens" in London (179). Comparable to Dracula's siphoning Lucy's life blood and the wolves killing the mother of the girl, Suzanne's husband, she learns, *"became violently ill"* after he *"was poisoned with filicin"* (180). Later, she has to confront the death of her daughter Rachel in a car accident. Reading and living in a Dracula-haunted world while waiting for David, Suzanne becomes "delirious" (179). Intensifying her torments, Dr. Freudenberger's reading sessions recall the pain of shifting identities in *Funnyhouse of a Negro* and *The Owl Answers*.

Undoubtedly, *Dracula* is the main "adapted" text in Suzanne's frightening film club of her life in 1961, but it is not the only one. As in *Funnyhouse of a Negro,* Kennedy uses Queen Victoria and key London locations to express her heroine's plight. Visiting "Windsor in the rain," Suzanne chronicles that "Queen Victoria had grieved for Albert there" and immediately injects her own concern about David. "My husband, where was he?" (176). Then her mind takes audiences to the Accra garden where David read "the love poems of Senghor" to her. But in the harrowing purgatory of Suzanne's London, Victoria is ultimately reduced to "a tiny, sad figure" (176), and replacing Suzanne's happy memories of the African garden is the London landscape filled with rain, "dark, curved street[s]," and the hectic nightly train rides. In this feverish and sickly London, Alice is often out of breath, and Suzanne's physical symptoms —asthma, nausea—accompany her psychic traumas.

In addition to suffering in the forlorn Victorian London of *Dracula,* Suzanne is traumatized by other texts. Throughout *The Film Club,* as Suzanne reads from Alice's letters to David, we hear about her futile shuttles to the American Express office in London hoping to have a word from him, and hear a grim newspaper account of David's poisoning in Geneva and Fanon's death in Washington, D.C., after Suzanne returns alone to the States. She confronts the ultimate horror when she tells us of Fanon: "I still read from his life and search for the cause of his illness and death" (180). Equally bleak, the romantic Alice has died, and "several years ago at Thanksgiving we looked for Alice's favorite scene of *Now, Voyager,* it was missing. She believed she lost it that winter in London" (180). In Suzanne's film club, her own favorite scene as a voyager is also missing. That fatal winter she nearly lost her husband and her mind, not to mention a great national leader. Yet glimmers of resistance appear in the short passage from Fanon that Suzanne reads in closing *The Film Club*: "*the war goes / on and we will have to bind . . . [the] ineffaceable wounds*" that the colonialist has "*inflicted on our / people*" (181).

Dramatic Circle

Dramatic Circle continues and completes Suzanne Alexander's three-week plight waiting for her husband's return from his near-death imprisonment in Africa. Commissioned by WNYC as a radio play in 1991, *Dramatic Circle,* like *The Film Club,* is filled with nightmares, violence, submerged and borrowed identities, and embedded scripts. Such horrors are conveyed verbally, not visually, in the tradition of such mystery radio shows of the 1930s and 1940s as *The Shadow,* but with a distinctive Kennedy stamp. Among the voices we hear are those of Suzanne, her sister-in-law Alice, Dr. Freudenberger, the ambassador who recounts the "plot against [Suzanne's] husband" (194), David (appropriately, a radio is the only source of information on him), and Napoleon and Josephine, from whose letters about their own separation Suzanne reads as a reflection of her tragedy. Passages from Bram Stoker's *Dracula* are also interspersed with dialogue from Kennedy's play.

In London, Suzanne is "nearly delirious" worrying about David and has "inexplicable dreams of historical characters and speaks as the characters [Napoleon and Josephine] in her sleepwalking" (185). In her fusion of identities, she recalls such

Kennedy characters as Sarah or Clara. Worried about her sister-in-law, Alice takes her to see Dr. Freudenberger, the young German psychiatrist who, as a part of his treatment of Suzanne, and as a welcome "distraction," invites them both to join a dramatic circle at his home where "all the participants were his patients . . . sitting in a circle" (187) reading from famous literary works, including *Dracula.* As in *The Film Club,* Suzanne is given the part of Lucy. Kennedy's title *Dramatic Circle* describes Freudenberger's gathering, but also points to David's eventual return to Suzanne, whom he left in *She Talks to Beethoven.* Their lives come full circle as Suzanne regains her psychic health and as David comes to her after being tortured in Ghana. Yet hearing that Lucy was "buried in a churchyard near Hampstead Heath," Alice admits, "The passage made me cry. We broke the circle . . . and said good night" (193). In their reunion, Suzanne and David also break their circle of torment.

But most of the play is taken up with the bizarre encounters between Suzanne and Dr. Freudenberger. Besides visiting him at his office and his home, she reveals, "I feel like I've seen him somewhere before" (189), further complicating the mystery of Kennedy's radio play. We learn that secretly, at night, Freudenberger "walked in the garden [where Suzanne was staying], limping, hair white, almost as an apparition" (196). At first skeptical, Alice later "was convinced" (193) and confronts Freudenberger. Taken with Suzanne's "fragile beauty," he confesses she was "going through bad times and . . . like Lucy, would become the victim of an unfair, tragic plot." Consequently, he disguised himself "to prepare Suzanne's mind for the darkness . . . she must face" (196). Though his Jungian methods are extreme, Freudenberger, unlike the sinister doctors of radio mysteries, wants to cure his patient. He is symbolically linked to another psychiatrist-hero, Frantz Fanon, David's friend who attempted to treat the "disorders" of political prisoners and worked for his country's independence. Unlike Freudenberger, who succeeded with Suzanne, David, sadly, could not "find the source of Frantz Fanon's illness" but does write a "powerful" biography of the revolutionary leader.

Yet other parallels exist between Freudenberger and characters in the Alexander plays. Like Beethoven, he becomes one of Suzanne's protectors and encouragers by cautioning her to rest, warning her about the risks of losing her child, and caring for her mental health. He is, as Alice admits, "a charming friend to us." No earlier Kennedy heroine can claim such a guardian. But, even more important, he shows how identities, like lines from Napoleon's letters or passages from *Dracula,* overlap in *Dramatic Circle.* His disguise in the garden is a pivotal element in Kennedy's fascination with the transformations of identity. In acting like an apparition, Freudenberger helps to secure or redeem the identities of Suzanne and David as wife and husband, much as Beethoven did in *She Talks to Beethoven.* Just as the great composer represented (and even sounded like) David until he returned, Freudenberger becomes David's proleptic substitute by disguising himself to look like David upon his return to London. As Alice recounts, "I hardly recognized David, he had changed so. He limped like an old man and his black hair had turned white" (196). Fittingly, this play also closes with the Fanon quotation that marks the end of *The Film Club* and with assurances that, even though David is now "lost in Blida" with Fanon, he will recover. Suzanne is well on her way on that journey thanks to a German-born London psychiatrist, who doubtless enjoyed Beethoven.

The Ohio State Murders

The Ohio State Murders is the longest of the Alexander plays, and regarded as one of Kennedy's best. In this play, Suzanne dredges up the traumatic memories that haunted Kennedy at Ohio State University, the occasion that constitutes the genesis and the frame for the script. Invited back to her alma mater to "talk about the violent imagery in [her] work; bloodied heads, severed limbs, dead father, dead Nazis, dying Jesus" (152), Suzanne remembers through a series of "dramatized flashbacks"[6] projecting the people, places, and events of forty years earlier as she rehearses her lecture on the O level of the library behind the stadium. She travels through a dreamscape during which we hear the voices from her past and catch a glimpse of their faces. In narrating these events, Suzanne relives the tragic murder of her twin daughters and the terrifying loss of her own innocence.

The Ohio State Murders premiered 5 March 1992 at the Great Lakes Theater Festival in Cleveland. The production, which ran through 22 March, was the first Kennedy play to be performed in her hometown. Gerald Freedman directed Ruby Dee as Suzanne Alexander, Bellary Darden as the young Suzanne, and Allan Byrne as the vile Professor Hampshire. Freedman astutely described Kennedy's canon as "dark and mysterious and strangely innocent, like the vision of a soulful child," a marvelous assessment of Suzanne's world in *The Ohio State Murders*. Summing up his response to the play, he continued: "You let it work on your unconscious and learn to trust on an imaginative level beyond the logical and rational,"[7] exactly the effect Kennedy sought. *The Ohio State Murders* immerses audiences in "dark landscapes" of place and mind.

The play originated in Kennedy's experiences as a student between 1949 and 1953. In an interview in the *Lantern,* the

Ohio State newspaper, she confessed: "I wouldn't walk on the campus for more than 30 years after graduation. . . . When I did grab a cab to visit OSU again, I found myself crying. I was stunned. The campus was so full of memories, so many emotional scenes." The ultimate cause of Kennedy's sorrow was, as she expressed, "a sense I got at OSU for the first time [in 1949] that Blacks were hated. It marks me to this day."[8] In another interview, Kennedy disclosed: "Thirty percent of it is totally true . . . the rest is imagination. In 1950, Ohio State was a landscape for racial hatred. I was used to living in a middle-class family in an immigrant and black neighborhood—two communities balancing themselves. Suddenly at Ohio State, it was a shock—12 black girls in a dorm, and people did not like blacks. We were maybe—I can't swear to it—less than 500 out of 25,000—a tiny number and disdained. In some funny way, I always wanted to answer to that. And I never got a handle on it until I went back to give a talk about tapping into the source of violence in my own work."[9] What would become *The Ohio State Murders* festered in her memory until, as she said, "I saw myself as this 18-year old girl in her saddle oxfords and I realized that racially divided atmosphere had affected me deeply. When I am distressed, things happen and images and ideas for the play began pouring out of me." "It was then," as Kennedy lamentably concluded, "that I tried to capture the feeling of violence through the use of imagery in a fictionalized story about an English professor who eventually murders [Suzanne's] twins."[10]

Suzanne, like Kennedy, discovers that "race was foremost" at Ohio State (154). And like Sarah in *Funnyhouse of a Negro* and Clara in *The Owl Answers*, she is branded inferior, rejected by the dominant white culture. Hoping to major in English literature, she was shocked that "there were no 'Negro' students in the English Department. It was thought that we were not able to master the program. They would allow you to take no more than two required freshman courses. After that you had to apply to the English Department to take courses that were all said to be for majors" (154). The dorms were also fiercely segregated: "white girls gave parties . . . but we were never invited" (164). Black students were forced to eat at separate tables or ate hamburgers at "Tomaine Tommie's" (157), a location as symbolically lethal as the dorm. As Suzanne later recalled, white girls like Bunny Manley "refused to speak to Iris and me and accused us of stealing her watch. . . . If they saw us coming down the corridor, they would giggle and close their door. I hated them. Their way of laughing when they saw us coming into the lounge, and then [their] refusal to speak was a powerful language. It had devastated me" (167). The racially divided campus, "choreographed visually through segregated geography,"[11] was disquieting for the young Suzanne. "The geography made me anxious" (152). Each place was fixed as white or "Negro"— "The zigzagged streets beyond the Oval were regions of Law, Medicine . . . the lawn behind the dorm where the white girls sunned. The ravine that would be the scene of the murder and Mrs. Tyler's boarding house in the Negro district" (152). Suzanne ominously divulges, "Very few Negroes walked on High Street above the university."

In a graphic example of racism at Ohio State, Suzanne recalls, "I was often so tense that I wound the plastic pink curlers in my hair so tightly that my head bled. When I went to the university health center, the white intern tried to examine my head and at the same time not touch my scalp or hair" (168). Again, she is reduced to an unclean untouchable by the prejudiced white world. Her body is a text written in rejection. This incident, or one like it perhaps, could have been the genesis for the bleeding heads, abhorred by the white establishment, in *Funnyhouse of a Negro*. Ultimately, Suzanne is expelled because of her writing, and again racism is responsible. In an unconscionable act of censorship, Miss Dawson, "head of the dorm . . . read my diaries to the dormitory committee and decided I was unsuitable. I did not fit into campus life." Moreover, Suzanne records, after the "baby was born I would not be allowed to return to campus" (161). Prejudice, writing, the plight of the artist, fatal love affairs, hair, blood, shadows, and deaths became the subjects and images that occupied Suzanne Alexander, as well as her creator Adrienne Kennedy.

As in her other plays, *The Ohio State Murders* presents Kennedy through multiple representations—she is both the older Suzanne Alexander who reflects on her past and the younger Suzanne who enacts it onstage. Consistent with Kennedy's artistic purpose, *The Ohio State Murders* explores black female identity in a white world through highly symbolic confrontations between the white establishment and a young and talented black woman. Unlike her other plays, though, *The Ohio State Murders* is, according to Kennedy, "more straightforward, more centered."[12] The present "slips" into the past as it does elsewhere in her canon, but the shifts are less graphic, less violent. *The Ohio State Murders* is "markedly less frenetic" than Kennedy's earlier work, a "quietly horrific tale of love and destruction."[13] In a sense, *The Ohio State Murders* supplements Kennedy's autobiography, *People*, but also looks forward to *Sleep Deprivation Chamber* in its reportorial techniques. Undeniably, *The Ohio State Murders* is one of Kennedy's most revelatory plays since it shows why she became a writer and how her work emerged from the shadows of her past.

Kennedy has always forged an intimate relationship with her characters. She is reflected in Suzanne, who is described in the script as "the young writer as a student attending Ohio State from 1949 to 1950." Like the student, Kennedy married a man who, just like David in *The Ohio State Murders,* became a civil rights activist and Fanon's biographer. (Unlike Suzanne, though, Kennedy never was expelled from Ohio State, nor did she get pregnant there.) The older Suzanne also had much in common with Kennedy as "a well-known black writer visiting Ohio State to give a talk on the imagery in her work" (151). Each woman carried traumatic memories from the experiences of those years. Examining the same stage of Suzanne's life, Kennedy was in her fifties when *The Ohio State Murders* was performed. Both the real and the fictive women wrote plays energized by violent imagery. Not surprisingly, much productive ambiguity resides in Kennedy's using the word "present" to denote the "well-known" writer and thus differentiate her from the student in the dialogue of *The Ohio State Murders.*

But these two Suzannes, older and younger, function more intricately than just as simple portraits of Kennedy, and Suzanne Alexander is far more complex than simply being Kennedy's "transparent alter ego."[14] They go beyond being mere fictionalized representations of her. In developing these characters, Kennedy continued experimenting with the performance of interior/exterior selves. *The Ohio State Murders* presents two voices and two different speakers/characters who are the same person. These characters are legitimate, not distorted or schizophrenic, claimants to Suzanne's psyche. A younger and an older Suzanne exist as separate characters but share the same experiences, either retrospectively or proleptically. As Ruby Dee pointed out about the play as well as the character she portrayed: "It's a journey of a woman into herself."[15] *The Ohio State Murders* joins other Kennedy plays as emanating from a character's mind, but multiplies by two the dramatic representations of that psyche. According to Freedman, "A lot of the activity [in the play] is internal."[16] We are invited to accompany Suzanne Alexander on her journey into self, past and present.

The ways characters appear and recede in Suzanne's memory reflect the journeys to the remote regions, the dark mystery unfolding on stage. Paula Maggio describes the process: "As Suzanne pulls them out of her memory into the light of recollection, the figures move in and out of the shadows on the darkened stage behind her. From the recesses of Suzanne's mind, they silently step out of the blackness into the spotlight as she thinks about the roles they played in her past."[17] The spotlight, as in Tennessee Williams's *Small Craft Warnings* (1972), becomes the perfect site—physically and psychically—for the confessional arias of Suzanne's memory play. Some characters make several, though brief, appearances—Hampshire, the professor, Iris, David, Mrs. Tyler, Aunt Louise. And a few appear just once or twice for only a snippet of dialogue—Mrs. Dawson, or Val, Suzanne's black date who never returned to her life. Sometimes we do not see a character but hear only a voice, a technique found in film noir as well. These bodiless voices forebodingly point to the absences Suzanne will have to accept in her life. Finally, some characters are neither seen nor heard, but only heard of, such as Bunny Manley.

Kennedy realizes these relationships in *The Ohio State Murders* by reenacting and dissecting Suzanne's life story through a narrative of voices that are heard "waiting, dreading, hoping, remembering, and reading. . . . Since nothing happens in the dramatized present, spectators must create a dramatic context."[18] The two Suzannes are vital to the process of remembering and creating drama. The voice of the student is innocent, romantic, vulnerable. Living in the very past being reenacted in the present, she exists in a time frame that unfolds with harrowing twists and turns, betrayals, and murders. The voice of Suzanne the writer in the present is knowledgeable, tested, and reasoned by pain, both past and present; she is the narrator/ writer of her own mystery story. Strengthened by an enduring pain, Suzanne Alexander strips away the layers of time, the accretions of memories over pain, to inform her audience—in the theater and in the Ohio State lecture hall—about the origins of violent imagery in her plays. That journey is cyclical, psychic; the last line of the play has Suzanne (and her audience) travel full circle: "And that is the main source of the violent imagery in my work" (173). As a survivor, the older Suzanne protects and preserves the younger woman as writer and actor. If Suzanne as student is the victim, then the older Suzanne Alexander is the vindicator. The relationship between the two suggests that of sisters, demanding comparison with Suzanne's murdered twin daughters (Carol and Cathi) as well as the twins in *June and Jean in Concert.*

These two Suzannes can also represent the inner (hidden, untold) and the external (revealed, narrated) worlds or lives of the same woman. As both a character and a narrator in the same play, Suzanne Alexander might be likened to Tom Wingfield in Tennessee Williams's *Glass Menagerie,* a work that heavily influenced Kennedy's early play *Pale Blue Flowers.* Like Tom Williams (a.k.a. Tennessee Williams), Suzanne becomes a "well-known writer," but only after the events of the play she narrates have occurred. Like Tom Wingfield, the narrator/character in *The Glass Menagerie,* she does not follow the strict rules of time but reveals clues to the mystery before it happened, before it was encapsulated in her memory. As narrator, then, Suzanne Alexander is character, chorus, actor, and author. She both fast-forwards and rewinds time in her and the young Suzanne's same-life tragedy.

Like many Kennedy plays, *The Ohio State Murders* does not unfold in a sequential, comfortably chronological way that builds up to a climax. Instead, there is slippage, disorienting revelations we don't expect or are not ready for, as in the disclosures conveyed through voice-overs in film noir. Events are reported or wrenched out of the time frame in which they would have happened. The present enters the past. Cause and effect are reversed. Early in the writer Suzanne's monologue we find a probing illustration of how events are disengaged from sequential time in her memory. Speaking of campus locations, she discloses the following before the crimes happen:

> I never saw this ravine until the two days I visited Bobby [Hampshire] at his house (the ravine was where the faculty lived).
>
> A year and a half later one of my baby twin daughters would be found dead there. That was later.
>
> But in my freshman year the continuing happiness was Professor Hampshire's discussion of the Victorian novel. (154)

Yet, much later in the play, Suzanne Alexander in the present unsettles our understanding by confessing: "In the fall I returned to Columbus. I felt my baby's murderer was someone I knew" (167). As these examples show, the disclosures and retracings in the plot emphasize the fragmentation the young Suzanne suffered and the splintered memories these events hold for the older

Suzanne now. Time is out of joint in *The Ohio State Murders,* and it is only Suzanne's memory that sets the record straight.

In another instance of reversing chronological time, immediately before we see the young Suzanne in Hampshire's office for the first time, the older Suzanne forebodingly reveals a major event resulting from that meeting: "For a long time no one knew who the killer was. She was the one I had called Cathi. But that was later" (155). Hence, before the crime is revealed in terms of a plot from the past, Suzanne in the present quietly slips in the key to the mystery. In the midst of her recollections of how Hampshire read *Beowulf* "so eloquently," she tells us: "Then it happened. Near the beginning of March Robert Hampshire kidnapped and murdered our daughter. She was the one called Cathi. He drowned her in the ravine" (165). This sudden, shocking revelation forces audiences to confront the terror that crept into Suzanne's life. By rearranging time Kennedy offers "an aesthetic puzzle for our minds to piece together,"[19] and a moral one, too.

Manipulating psychic time, the older Suzanne then comments, in a terrifyingly simultaneous present, on the actions we have just witnessed between the student Suzanne and Hampshire forty years ago—"He didn't seem to hear me"—as if to give voice to the student who was not empowered to speak these words to him or to anyone else at Ohio State in 1949. Years later, the older Suzanne voices the intimate thoughts that the younger woman kept to herself. "I became pregnant the following Christmas, 1950. My parents thought I spent the last day of the break with Iris in Akron, but I had come back to Columbus and spent two days with Bobby above the ravine" (160). Taking us back in both psychic and chronological time, Suzanne the writer a few minutes later confesses: "Seeing Bobby read made me brood over how he had dismissed me. Why?" (165).

As the example shows, this "well-known writer" often responds to or comments on an event or a recollection of dialogue after the younger Suzanne has said or done something. But Kennedy varies this pattern, too. The older Suzanne says, "Easter was when I told my father that I had been dismissed from the dorm. He was sitting in the office at his church. Tears came into his eyes." And immediately thereafter we hear the young student recall, "Now sometimes on Sunday when I thought the campus was empty, I'd put the twins in Mrs. Tyler's coupe and drive to the river or the stadium . . . and try to figure out what I was going to do with my life" (164). Moving from present to past and then back to the present, Kennedy involves the audience in the mystery of Suzanne's life. We become entangled in the darkness with her. As we move closer to the end of the play, we hear more and more from the writer Suzanne, as character, narrator, and conscience.

Another way Kennedy deepens her character's tragedy in *The Ohio State Murders* is by inserting passages from parallel literary works reverberating with relevance for Suzanne. In earlier works, Kennedy often quoted from one or more of her own plays—lines from *The Owl Answers* appear in *Movie Star* and passages from *A Rat's Mass* and *The Owl Answers* are embedded in *June and Jean in Concert*. But in *The Ohio State Murders* she does not cite her own work, but, rather, includes Hampshire reading from *Tess of the D'Urbervilles*, Thomas Hardy's 1891 novel of an innocent country girl who is seduced by a corrupt rogue, Alec D'Urberville, a would-be member of the gentry. Tess conceives and gives birth to a child out of wedlock with Alec, but the baby dies. Hoping to escape Alec, Tess flees and falls in love with Angel Clare, but ends up killing Alec so she can enjoy, though briefly, Angel's love.

The links between Tess's fate and Suzanne's are many and complex. Like Tess, Suzanne is seduced and then trapped by a cruel society that Hampshire, like Alec, symbolizes. Both women break the codes of this dominant society and are punished for it. Hampshire's interpretation of the social context of Hardy's work also evocatively applies to Suzanne's condition at Ohio State: "The net narrows and finally closes. Inherent in almost all Hardy's characters are those natural instincts which become destructive because social conventions suppress them, attempting to make the human spirit conform to the 'letter'" (155). Through social conventions Hampshire and Ohio State attempt to suppress Suzanne's spirit and make it conform to the letter of their punishing laws.

In juxtaposing Hardy's text with Suzanne's life story, Kennedy shows how Suzanne's tragedy is being absorbed into Tess's. Suzanne writes a paper on Tess for Hampshire, and he unwittingly remarks, "Paper has unusual empathy for Tess" (157). In class, he draws a map of the Wessex countryside where the novel takes place—"Blackmore, Vale, Marlott, Edgdon Heath, New Forest," names that ironically echo Suzanne's plight as a black student caught in the vale edges and dark forests of Ohio State. Further identifying herself with Tess, Suzanne draws maps of these tragic Hardy landscapes, which become part of the documents leading to her expulsion from Ohio State (161). On one level, then, Tess's tragedy is Suzanne's. But Kennedy does not permit a simple and clean identification between or equivalence of Tess and Suzanne. Unlike Tess, who kills Alec to get Angel back, Suzanne does not murder for love.

It is Hampshire, doubling as Alec in Kennedy's appropriation of Hardy's text, who murders—for hate, to kill love. Hampshire is no "Angel," which is what Suzanne so painfully learns after sitting in his class. In effect, then, Hampshire's reading of Hardy is a distortion of the novel in light of the tragedy that befalls Suzanne. Like Sarah or Clara Passmore, Suzanne becomes a victim of the white literary establishment.

Kennedy uses a second literary text to emphasize Suzanne's fate and Hampshire's deceit. After she has the twins and tries to "figure out what I was going to do with my life" (164), she slips into one of "Bobby's lectures" and hears him read from and interpret twenty-five lines of Tennyson's "King Arthur" in the "dimly lit auditorium." The passage is titled "Arthur Vows Revenge," after the death of his best friend Gawain in battle. Again, a literary occasion for mourning is juxtaposed against Suzanne's plight. An inconsolable Arthur is told by his followers, "Your cause of grief is cureless and cannot be remedied," an ironic counterpoint to Suzanne's hopelessness over Hampshire's betrayal. Arthur is admonished, "To weep like a woman is not judged wise" (164), linking the English king with Suzanne. Yet Arthur's grief over his friend's death profoundly contrasts this "manly monarch" with the shameless Hampshire, who can teach but not live a literary text of fidelity and sorrow in his own life. Because he does not "clamor for love," Hampshire becomes the antithesis of the heroic Arthur. Hampshire's interpretation of this passage is equally disgusting, stained with his self-preserving practicality: "Arthur's only expression of sin in the poem is touched off by his grief over Gawain. But perhaps it was a battle-sin of caution" since Arthur did not want to cross the "low water" that would have put him at "Gawain's side in the battle" (165). Cautious treachery is indeed Hampshire's sin.

Adding to the symbolism in *The Ohio State Murders* is the snow that *"falls throughout the play"* (152). The campus is marked by *"dark trees and snow"* (161), which falls when Suzanne discovers that Hampshire has kidnapped one of the twins. Reversing the traditional associations of snow with purity and goodness, Kennedy chillingly links snow with the heartless world of white oppression in which Suzanne finds herself, as well as the deathlike mantle in which her memories of Ohio State have been shrouded. Like the white imagery in Albert Camus's existential novel *The Stranger* or Tennessee Williams's late (first published in 1991) apocalyptic play *The Chalky White Substance,* snow symbolizes an existential void, a world deprived of caring. Additionally, the steadily falling snow acts like a measured dirge accompanying the numerous scene changes and deaths in the play. Analyzing the significance of snow and various other visual elements, Keith A. Joseph concludes:

> The play is not so much a dramatization, but a cacophony of verbal and visual images—a distorted nightmare. There are superimposed slides throughout the play, showing surrealistic images of books, the OSU campus, demonic figures coming to steal her baby and abstract flashes of red carnage. All of this surrounds a gigantic centerstage window showing a contrapuntal snowfall.[20]

The snow is silent, a deadly reminder of the violence surrounding Suzanne.

Psychological as well as physical violence haunt *The Ohio State Murders*. David Kornhaber perceptively separates these two types within the play: "Violence of sexual exploitation, kidnapping and murder are all forms of horror easily under-stood and condemned, even if they are impossible to describe in terms that do justice to the pain they can create." But, he argues, there is another type of violence, "the violence we don't know how to confront, the violence of exclusion—the violence of a system that forbids the brightest students from studying what they love, that purposely works its most promising talents to the point of exhaustion and despair. It is a subtle unspoken, cold kind of violence, all the more disturbing for its complete lack of passion."[21] This is the inner violence that Freedman had identi-fied in his "Director's Notes."

In his production of *The Ohio State Murders* in Cleveland, Freedman captured both the outer violence of kidnapping, stalking, and murder and the inner violence of despair and exclusion through a provocative set expressing the subterranean worlds of white and dark, shadows and reality, dreams and death, wombs and wounds. Behind Suzanne, as she reads, Freedman positioned two large screens projecting a host of images—photographs, key words, places, and icons. These two screens represented the two worlds in which Suzanne lived—the external and the internal—and the two time frames of the play. A picture of the library as Suzanne the student stands at the bot-tom of the building on one screen recalls events from the past, as Suzanne the writer stands before the audience surrounded by distorted images of books and their looming presence in her tragedy. In another instance, "footage of the film *Battleship Potemkin*" (159), which Iris and Suzanne watched, appears on one screen as we watch Suzanne's older self watch her younger self at the same event. These screens showed the layered worlds of dreams and performance that characterize Kennedy's earlier plays.

Sounds also shape an audience's perceptions of and fears for Suzanne. Off-stage noises take the place of visual representations of the heinous deeds that became the origin for the violent imagery in her works. Very little, in fact, is actually shown or dramatized in *The Ohio State Murders*. Sirens go off when the kidnapping occurs; gunshots are only heard when Suzanne reveals the deaths of her twin daughters or when suspects are mentioned. Audiences hear "the inane, hideous laughter of the white girls in Suzanne's dormitory"[22] after they spurn Suzanne in their culture of exclusivity. Widely different musical scores also resonate throughout *The Ohio State Murders*. Dorm music (158) and *"music from [the] corridor"* (163) include strains from *Oklahoma* and *Carousel*, light-hearted musicals contrasting with Suzanne's own sad music of loss.[23] Ironically, at the beginning of the play, Suzanne recalls one popular song, "Don't You Go 'Way Mad," which is later heard in her monologue. Yet audiences must ask themselves, how could Suzanne go away from Ohio State in any other way except with righteous but quiet anger and maddening memories?

CHAPTER 7

Kennedy's Political Morality Plays

Sun: A Poem for Malcolm X Inspired by His Murder,
An Evening with Dead Essex, Sleep Deprivation
Chamber, and *Motherhood 2000*

Coming of age during the civil rights movement, it is not surprising that Kennedy wrote plays that raise volatile political issues. Even in elementary school Kennedy thought of "Negroes": "We were underdogs, and underdogs must fight in life" (*People,* 11). Her scripts often revolve around a horrific political and historical event that has layers of psychic meaning for black characters in a world of white bigotry. For instance, the bloody assassination of Patrice Lumumba in the 1960s counterpoints the psychic horrors Sarah faces in a world of white Victorian power in *Funnyhouse of a Negro.* Nazi atrocities historicize the nightmares of *A Rat's Mass*'s Brother and Sister Rat. In *The Owl Answers,* Clara encounters infamy at the hands of an Anglo-Saxon culture quintessentially symbolized by William the Conqueror, among others. *The Ohio State Murders* is saturated with hate crimes, resulting in a child killing reminiscent of so many civil rights atrocities of the 1950s and 1960s.

Although politics, like dreams, forms the substrata of many of Kennedy's plays, four of them can be grouped overridingly as political morality plays—*Sun: A Poem for Malcolm X Inspired by His Murder, An Evening with Dead Essex, Sleep Deprivation Chamber,* and *Motherhood 2000.* Each concentrates on the tragic fate of a real-life young black man whose identity and worth are attacked by a racist society. Revealing Kennedy's political sympathies, these plays evolve from actual hate incidents, retelling traumatized histories. *Sun* focuses on the assassination of Malcolm X; *An Evening with Dead Essex* on the harrowing impact of the execution of a black Vietnam War veteran; *Sleep Deprivation Chamber* on the racial profiling of Kennedy's own son Adam; and *Motherhood 2000* on the mother's revenge for her son's tragedy in *Sleep Deprivation Chamber*. The black men and women of these plays enter surrealistic worlds where there is no difference between a nightmare and a historical incident.

Sun: A Poem for Malcolm X Inspired by His Murder

Sun premiered at the Royal Court Theatre in London in 1968 and was dedicated to Kennedy's father.[1] Ostensibly Kennedy's least overtly didactic political play, *Sun* nevertheless commemorates one of the most politicized black leaders of the 1950s and 1960s. Malcolm X (born Malcolm Little in 1925) was a revolutionary, charismatic prophet for the Nation of Islam who urged a separatist black state in America. A protégé of Elijah Muhammad, Malcolm X defected from the Nation of Islam in 1964 and became a target of both it and the FBI and CIA. He claimed that the black man in America had been stripped of his name, culture, and history by a colonizing white society,[2] a message consistent with the tragic lessons Kennedy's heroines learn.

Like Kennedy, Malcolm had visited Ghana and exhorted black Americans to be proud of their African heritage. Like Kennedy, too, he admired Patrice Lumumba and Kwame Nkrumah, Ghana's prime minister about whom Kennedy, when wearing "a skirt of the blue cloth with Nkrumah's face illustrated" on it, said, "I felt when I wore it that I sealed my ancestry as West African" (*People,* 122). Malcolm X confessed that "if I was in Africa I know I would be killed by the same people who killed Lumumba."[3] Prophetically, his own death was as brutal as Lumumba's. On 27 February 1965, three Nation of Islam messengers brutally shot Malcolm X fifteen times as he was preaching in New York City. Honoring Malcolm X as a black prophet and martyr, *Sun* can be read as a political allegory radically different in technique from Spike Lee's powerful film *Malcolm X* (1992) but similar in its appreciation of him.

Sun remains one of Kennedy's most poetic, experimental dramas. William R. Elwood labels it one of her "most hymnic works."[4] The play can be classified as a choreopoem, a poem written to be staged with an emphasis on music, drama, lighting, spectacle, and the fluidity of performance. *Sun* looks forward to the choreopoem *For Colored Girls Who Have Considered Suicide When the Rainbow Is Enuf* (1974) by Ntozake Shange, a playwright who has readily acknowledged her debt to Kennedy.[5] With its forceful emphasis on spectacle—e.g., orbiting suns and moons—and a highly lyrical libretto in nine different movements, *Sun* might also be compared to an opera. But the movements in *Sun* ignore and transcend time and plotted chronology. Or, as Elwood notes, "movement replaces time."[6] Essentially, though, *Sun* is a choreographed political requiem for the fallen black leader.

Malcolm X's life and death are symbolically conveyed through Kennedy's expressionistic cosmic setting and imagery. In this one-character drama, Man (Malcolm X) is surrounded by a steel wire around which various suns and moons revolve, flash, drop, disappear, and shatter. His fate is linked to these

various cosmic bodies. Man's body parts—head, arms, legs—
are fragmented; they float, orbit, and are *"blotted by blood"*
(60) in synchronicity with changes in the sun and the moon.
"Suddenly blood starts to run out of the fragmented moon"
(59) and then, correspondingly, in a later movement, *"In the
moon Man's body falls apart"* (61). *"A disembodied leg
appears, vanishes. In the third time suns explode over the whole
scene . . . blood stops pouring out of the fragmented moon"*
(59). Malcolm X's brutal shooting is unquestionably alluded to
through this explosive cosmic imagery. His lungs, arteries, limbs
are transformed and transcribed through these orbiting spheres.
"The position of the moon" and Man's disembodied head are
inextricably connected: *"The expression of the face of the head
changes. All of these changes seem to be felt within the Man
since they are his inner state"* (57). Kennedy's emphasis has
shifted from her heroines' inner selves to that of this political
leader.

The sun is the central symbol in Kennedy's eulogy. Long
an icon representing Christ (the sun/son of God), this celestial
body here represents Malcolm X, poetically and politically. But
Kennedy rhapsodically transforms this traditional symbol into a
multivalent field of references. Seeing himself a born prophet
and savior, Malcolm X affirms, "my mother dreamed she saw /
me in the sun" (57) and proclaims, "I felt myself / to be in the
midst of the sun" (56). As the play begins, a *"Red sun evolves.
. . . A yellow light. Half of the moon vanishes. He watches it
fearfully over his shoulder as the half slowly drifts away"* (56).
Then, more optimistically, an *"Orange sun spins . . . Yellow sun
now appears, spins. Beautiful sound."* The accompanying lines
spoken by Man read: "I like to think my heart / led to light."
Man exults, "As a young man I felt myself / to be in the midst

of the sun" (56), symbolically fusing Malcolm X's inner self with his public calling. In one of his speeches, Malcolm X in fact interpreted the battle for civil rights through sun imagery: "Fighting for our place in the sun, we will not rest until that place has been secured."[7]

But a progression of differently colored suns portends Man's subsequent agony and execution. As the suns change color, they foreshadow trouble in the heavens and on earth for the sun-anointed black leader. Man is vanquished in the struggle, reflected in both spectacle and image: "then the / sun went down and at / night I appear within the moon. . . . And as the moon / fragments and all is imbalanced / I keep on thinking of land-scapes" (58). The bright orange and yellow suns of promise turn to black—"the sun is now myself / dismembered in darkness / my blood my dismembered / self at sundown on the moon" (59). Then, "*Wire breaks. Flashing grey and black suns . . . Great collision, then the Man who is blotted out by the blood becomes smaller and smaller . . . and vanishes into a tiny red sun*" until "*red sun turns black*" and "*all vanishes . . . Except tiny black sun,*" and then even the Man's voice vanishes with this final incomplete sentence—"I still" (61), paradoxically both signaling the end of Malcolm's life and assuring the perpetuation of his memory. Ossie Davis, who delivered Malcolm X's eulogy, used the following sun imagery to describe the slain leader's impact on the world. "As the sun went down . . . we remembered something great and important to all of us that would not be back again."[8]

In addition to celestial imagery, Kennedy incorporates numerous Christian allusions to underscore Malcolm X's fame and fate as a savior. Like the suns and moons, Christian imagery in *Sun* moves freely from the birth to the death of Jesus, in whose image Man is cast. Opening with references to the magi, "the adoration of kings," and "a madonna and child" (55), *Sun* associates Malcolm's birth with Christ's. But by inserting a reference to a unicorn along with these images, Kennedy situates Man's beginnings in the world of the primeval, the fantastic. In the next few movements, *Sun* evolves, as in a horror fantasy, from the "embryo / in the uterus"—perhaps Malcolm X's "Annunciation"—to "a nude man / with his arms stretched out," an analogous visual image of the crucified Christ. The slain prophet is then linked with "a doomed / church . . . horses and riders" (57), further biblical imagery calling to mind Pharaoh and his horsemen, who perhaps echo the forces of evil metaphorically implicated in Malcolm X's death.

As in *Funnyhouse of a Negro* and *The Owl Answers,* images of heads play a major role in *Sun.* "The head of an apostle," the "head of the infant St. John," and the "head / of Infant Jesus" correlate with Man's own "dismembered head," linking Malcolm's martyrdom with the saintly apostles. The reference to Saint John may be to John the Baptist, who was beheaded. But, more certainly, Man's allusion to "the head of / an apostle" points to Saint James the Greater (Acts 12:1–2), Mathias (who replaced Judas), and Saint Paul, all of whom were beheaded for their faith. As the martyred prophet for black Americans, Malcolm X is torn apart for his faith in the cause.

An Evening with Dead Essex

Written in 1973 and first performed in 1974 at the Yale Repertory Theatre, where Adrienne Kennedy was a CBS Fellow in Playwrighting, *An Evening with Dead Essex* is one of her least appreciated works. It is also one of her most revolutionary plays, attacking in grim documentary detail racial prejudice by a white system of justice. In such a society, black men and women are the victimized minority. Kennedy declares, "I feel intensely that white American culture always . . . is trying to diminish black Americans. In ways that are subtle and ways that are not so subtle. So I always had to be a fighter."[9] *An Evening with Dead Essex* records Kennedy's anger at racism.

The play dramatizes the story of Mark James Essex, a Vietnam veteran who, in January 1973, shot six victims and wounded twelve others from atop the Downtown Howard Johnson Lodge in New Orleans until he was "trapped" in "a withering crossfire" between a police helicopter and "marksmen in two adjacent buildings" (125). Essex's life and death become the subjects of a small black theater group rehearsing a play about him to be performed the next day at a church in Harlem. The rehearsal we see and hear is really the play Kennedy has written about Essex. It is "a play about a play."[10] An improvisational, experimental, and episodic play, *An Evening with Dead Essex* comprises conversations among the director and actors of the play-within-the-play as they watch slides of Essex—from his boyhood in Kansas to his death from over one hundred police bullets. They shuffle through slides, posters, newspaper clippings, and blown-up photos as they comment on the man and the times.

An Evening with Dead Essex unfolds with a documentary realism that is very different from Kennedy's surrealistic nightmares about black women driven to madness and death. In fact, like agit-prop (propagandizing) plays of the 1930s, such as Clifford Odets's *Waiting for Lefty*, Kennedy's directs the actors "to use their real names and the director should get the actors to play themselves" (117). And at one point an actress and the director "*discuss a real current news item, if possible, one that day . . . reflecting violence*" (122). One production captured this tension in the script, as anger erupted when Gaby Rodgers, a white director at the American Place Theatre, was confronted by black actors who claimed she did not understand their "experience" in this play.[11]

As a testimonial play, *An Evening with Dead Essex* also demands comparison with documentary dramas of the 1970s such as Emily Mann's *Execution of Justice* (about Dan White murdering the mayor of San Francisco). In its documentary style and content, *An Evening with Dead Essex* looks toward the horrific incidents in *The Ohio State Murders* and *Sleep Deprivation Chamber*. *An Evening with Dead Essex* also joins American plays on Vietnam, i.e., David Rabe's *Sticks and Bones* and *Streamers*. As a victim of that war, Essex saw deception all around him. He trusted "the white faces" he knew in Kansas, but in Vietnam he bonded with "a darker brother for a country that despises him even more than his Viet Nam enemy" (120). According to the director, Viet Nam, with "nearly two tons of bombs" dropped on it, and the Howard Johnson rooftop where "police kept firing even after [Essex] went down, his body twitching with the impact of each slug . . . [are] one and the same" (125). For Essex, the war never left home.

Yet Kennedy's play is "as much about the theater company as it is Mark Essex."[12] During rehearsal, the director and the actors project images of Essex that they want to investigate, inscribe, and inhabit. Their comments, fears, bonds, and animus uncover Essex's multiple selves. "Remember this," insists the director to his actors, an admonition Kennedy gives her audiences as well. The divisions between acting and living, nightmare and reality, dissolve. The actors are "people under pressure," revealing Essex's feelings and struggles. Their pressure exerts its force on an audience that must relive the events leading up to the shooting. *An Evening with Dead Essex* takes us into the nightmare through clippings, slides, and posters. In the Yale production, "placards laid up against a wall depict a legless Black G.I., scrawny Vietnamese children running from a napalm attack, along with advertisements for a fur sale at Bergdoff-Goodman."[13] But Kennedy's dramaturgy is more complex than simple surface realism suggests. Essex's story—his political nightmare—exists on three levels: (1) as it was reported in the news (raw documents); (2) as his thoughts, which could not be incorporated into news stories; and (3) as the man he is perceived to be and lionized as by the acting company.

An Evening with Dead Essex thus exemplifies Kennedy's metatheater, exploring the idea of theater and performance, how a character is perceived and what that character's selves say about an interior history. Mel Gussow claims that *An Evening with Dead Essex* "describe[s] a thought process."[14] Although on the surface it seems like a discussion about historical documents, the play interrogates the way images are put together. Kennedy's set—a studio in a film company—is scattered with the props of image making, taking, recording, and replaying, in a *"Screening room . . . [with] Screen, projector, Posters rolled, and stacked in shelves, Tape recorder." "The floor should be black . . . except for glaring silver film cans and white-rolled up posters"* (117–18). Typical of both Kennedy's earlier plays and film noir, *An Evening with Dead Essex* is set in a shadowy world, an *"area made to look enclosed and dim except for one center glaring ceiling light."* The rehearsal occurs from *"late afternoon,"* to *"evening,"* to *"night,"* simulating the encroaching dark world of the Essex nightmare in American history.

Kennedy's play presents the man through his various selves in a radicalization of history, giving us a larger, even more troubling consciousness of Essex. "We have a lot to say about dead

Essex" (119–20), claims one of the black actors. They (re)shoot Essex's life, giving us multiple perspectives of his collective self as a patriotic boy in Kansas, a serviceman whose fears are expressed by ex-servicemen, a boy in a church, the young man who recited the Twenty-third Psalm and sang "My Country 'Tis of Thee," a black soldier in a revolutionary cause, a man who lived in a hovel on Dryades Street, and a fugitive being ripped apart. The actors' goal is to get inside Essex, to understand and convey "everything that preyed on his unconsciousness—not things that happened to him but all that was around him—his witnessing the loss of love—the loss of Christ" (123). They even compare him to a hero, to Christ. The director steadfastly reveals a Kennedyesque obsession with interior states, but in an unremittingly politicized environment.

The frequency and importance of the slides, photographs, and posters further contribute to unraveling Essex's multiple selves. The visual "clutter" in the rehearsal room becomes the map to his interior self as well as to his enemies. A white projectionist, who has no dialogue, is responsible for showing the slides at the director's request. Ironically, history is recorded and filtered through a white man concerned only with facts endorsing a dominant society's interpretation. Yet the order of and commentary on these slides and photos suggests a black penetration into history, as *Sun* does regarding Malcolm X. The result is a reordering of events for a much more complex picture of Essex. Trying to get inside Essex's head, the director orders the projectionist to "flash Essex as a boy." Then the director "*studies it. A long time,*" and shouts, "The focus isn't right—get it bigger" (121). "Stop on Essex's mother . . . closer—a little further away—bring it back a little" (118). "Flash Essex a boy large" (122). Photos flash and slides click in a dizzying array. We see the white faces Essex grew up with—"*a teacher of Essex looking at his year book. Two wounded policemen in New Orleans*" (125).

Yet the written record, slides, photos, and posters tell only part of Essex's life. In their obsessively random appearances, these images help create an impression but do not bring closure. We see images of Essex, his face, his eyes, his bullet holes, his boyhood friends and places, all those stimuli that "preyed upon his consciousness," but we rarely hear him, save for the actors performing the Twenty-third Psalm or intoning Essex's anger by reading slogans found in his room. Although we are led to put him at the center of the play that bears his name, Essex's identity is found only in fleeting performance. His memory is inscribed in the memories of the actors who call upon us "remember this," which is not easy, simple, or sequential. *An Evening with Dead Essex* is a political nightmare revealed in double exposure—we glimpse both an interior tragedy and see and external one. But unlike the horrors that Sarah or Clara Passmore experienced, Essex's made the headlines in every major newspaper in America.

Sleep Deprivation Chamber

Like *An Evening with Dead Essex*, *Sleep Deprivation Chamber*, which won an Obie in 1996, is based on a real incident in the life of Kennedy's son Adam, who coauthored the play with her. Adam P. Kennedy is a writer and producer whose programs—for instance, "Africa/US: The Connection"—have appeared on PBS and on network television. Late on the evening of 11 January 1991, his car was followed for several blocks by an Arlington, Virginia, policeman because of a faulty taillight. When

Adam Kennedy pulled into the driveway of his father's home, the officer brutally beat him without provocation and arrested him without specifying the charge. Unjustly accused of resisting arrest and assaulting an officer, Kennedy was the one sent to the hospital with multiple bruises, while the policeman produced no evidence of having been injured. The charges against Kennedy were dropped after a trial, and he won a civil suit against Arlington County. *Sleep Deprivation Chamber* dramatizes the events of that January night as well as the subsequent interrogations, conferences, and, finally, the trial. Kennedy appears as Suzanne Alexander and Adam is represented by the character Teddy. As Suzanne, Kennedy records many of the events in the play in "Letter to My Students on My Sixty-first Birthday by Suzanne Alexander" (*Kennedy Reader*, 197–227).

In both its subject matter and its approach, *Sleep Deprivation Chamber* is indebted to several types of theater as well as film. As Robert Vorlicky points out, "the play strikes close to the heart of the tradition of American domestic family drama."[15] It shows how a father, a sister, a community, and most of all a mother, who is also a writer, bond to protect a son. *Sleep Deprivation Chamber* shares traits with courtroom plays and films as varied as Barrie Stavis's *Lamp at Midnight*, about Galileo's trial, and Herman Wouk's *Caine Mutiny Court-Martial*. Elements of film noir—shadows, crimes, voice-overs—also help define *Sleep Deprivation Chamber*. Still other influences shaped the script, as Adrienne Kennedy's comments on the play's emergence suggest:

> Adam sent me his depositions, a police manual, and some of his own writings on the incident. Looking over all this material, I realized that there was a play here. I had written a piece for a literary magazine called "Letter to My Students," about

my anxieties during that time. So Adam and I put all these elements together. It's a moral victory to us that all these bits and pieces found their way into some kind of statement about the case.[16]

The play that resulted from this mosaic of evidence and anxiety was indeed a "moral victory" against the forces of racism that Kennedy had been battling since *Funnyhouse of a Negro*. *Sleep Deprivation Chamber* is a play about witnessing racial injustice. Recognizing its advocacy for the oppressed, Theater Emory in Atlanta staged a production of *Sleep Deprivation Chamber* to benefit the American Civil Liberties Union Foundation in 2001.

In obsessive, gruesome detail, the play documents the tragedy of racial profiling, the pernicious train of thought that links blacks with crime and thereby stereotypes them, "justifying" the police stopping and interrogating African Americans much more often than white citizens.[17] In an interview six years before *Sleep Deprivation Chamber* was produced, and only a year before the incident involving her son, Kennedy nailed the danger of such racial profiling:

I have been more haunted and obsessed in recent years with how the media treats blacks . . . in the media, blacks have become very much identified with drugs and a lot of negative things, and I don't remember that being [so] in the forties or fifties or the sixties. I am really worried about that. I don't know how that happened. The average black family is hardworking and has a very high morality.[18]

Stigmatizing blacks as a threatening presence has a long, painful history in America, as a letter in the play from Suzanne to the

Governor of Virginia attests. Pleading for help for her son Teddy, she compares the police brutality he experienced to "the persecution" of a black man "in the Deep South in the 1930's or during Emmett Till's time" (8).[19] A fourteen-year-old black boy, Till was savagely murdered in segregated Mississippi in 1955 for presumably flirting with a white woman. His death—his mutilated body was thrown into the Tallahatchie River—and the acquittal of his white murderers shocked the nation and significantly influenced the civil rights movement. A filmlike flashback in scene 3 of *Sleep Deprivation Chamber* about Teddy and his cousin being harassed in Los Angeles just a few years before Teddy's trial similarly typifies the evils of racism, particularly racial profiling. When Teddy and his cousin asked police for directions, the officers unjustifiably pulled them out of their car, "threw them against the wall," put a gun "against Teddy's temple," and shouted: "What are you doing in this part of town?" and "Nigger, I'll blow your head off. Where did you get the Jaguar?" (50).

In attacking police violence against African Americans in the 1990s, *Sleep Deprivation Chamber* participates in and continues the civil rights struggles of the 1960s. When the play was staged at Boston's Northeastern University in 2000, audiences "waiting for the play to begin" were "hypnotized through a compilation of speeches by Martin Luther King, Malcolm X, JFK, and other civil rights activists that set the premise for the play."[20] Neither Adam's/Teddy's education nor his standing as a respected son of a prominent family could protect him from racial profiling in Arlington, Virginia, in 1991. *Sleep Deprivation Chamber* also calls to mind the brutal treatment Rodney King received from the Los Angeles police in 1991 or "the shooting . . . by a policeman of a black man in Queens as he sat in his sister's car in front of his own house."[21] In "A Letter to My Students," Kennedy as Suzanne writes: "I made a list of black mothers whose sons were beaten by the police" (214). Teddy bewails this tragedy of American (in)justice when he is told, despite proof of his innocence, that he may go to jail. "I don't think I heard anything else after that. Here I was thinking that I was embarking upon the trail of vindication and justice. And they were about to send me on the expressway to Lorton Prison. What the hell happened to innocent till proven guilty? This was more like guilty till proven guiltier" (*Sleep Deprivation Chamber*, 19–20). In a lamentably symbolic incident, Teddy's Uncle Marsh, a civil rights leader, "disappears and wanders in the Palo Alto hills." When Teddy comments that Marsh "suffers memory lapses and . . . seems forgotten by younger activists" (15), we mourn the loss of earlier civil right victories.

As in other Kennedy plays, characters in *Sleep Deprivation Chamber* are submerged inside a nightmare filled with violence, a world gone mad. Events occur "in the middle of the night [on] a dead end street" (45) or in a covert legal system where an "Unseen Questioner" (33) or "unseen Lawyer for the prosecution" (13) contribute to the mystery, and to the Alexanders' dread. As in a macabre film noir, deprived of sleep, we are up all night like the characters, battling hallucinations. Teddy relives the horrors of his arrest, and his mother accompanies him in her own surrealistic fantasies and fears. "Less than five minutes of horror was turning into a never-ending nightmare. A nightmare so terrifying that no matter how much I screamed, I couldn't wake" (20), as Teddy declares. Later, he reveals, "I would never hit a police officer I . . . the nightmares" (47). But, as Ben Brantley observed, the "'funnyhouse of a Negro' has shifted from a haunted interior landscape to a world that is crushingly real. . . .

This is the stuff of nightmares from which a person can never wake up completely."[22]

In this externalized nightmare setting, the police inflict torture. Police brutality and a justice system shielding them turn Teddy's life, and his family's, upside down, inside out. "Few people win cases against the police," warns Teddy's attorney, Edelstein (25). *Sleep Deprivation Chamber* is packed with violent imagery and events gushing from police beatings and cover-ups. Again and again, we are told that Officer Holzer "sucker punched" Teddy—hit him in the face with a flashlight, and beat him raw. "The officer was pushing me on top of the car and because I had been kicked in the chest I had a very difficult time breathing" (33). Witnessing his son's beating, David Alexander testified, "It was like chaos" (29). Whether his assault is acted expressionistically or through actual physical encounters in production, Teddy writhes in pain from punches; his body contorts and recoils from being pushed, dragged, bloodied. His torture is gut-wrenching.

In this suffocating world, painted in blood and bruises, *Sleep Deprivation Chamber* reenacts how a black family suffers with a racist white world denying them justice and dignity. The play is like a dark sequel to Kennedy's family scrapbook, *People*. The Alexanders (Kennedys) are the target of bloody violence in word and deed. In fact, a bull's-eye target appears on the cover of the Theatre Communications Group edition of the play, and a circle resembling the barrel of a gun is drawn around the word *Sleep* on the title page. The title itself of the play is visually rendered ambiguous—the Alexanders are put in the sights of a gun chamber by living in a horror chamber of justice in sleep-depriving Arlington, Virginia.

Sleep Deprivation Chamber thrusts a disjuncted political narrative at audiences. Testimony about the incident does not unfold in a chronological, straightforward way. In typical Kennedy fashion, information is fragmented, interrupted. The incident (or parts of it) is played, replayed, remembered, inter-rogated, and reinterrogated. Caught up in the panic and the rage pulsating under the surface of legal proceedings, an audience has to sort out, rearrange, and relive the bits and pieces out of which the play was composed, each time becoming a little more disoriented, dislocated, panic-stricken. Times and places are spliced, conflated, intermixed, juxtaposed. *Sleep Deprivation Chamber* jolts audiences back and forth between Arlington in 1991, Aurora and Cleveland, Ohio, in the 1940s (where Suzanne grew up), Stanford in 1989 (where Suzanne teaches), Los Angeles in the 1980s (where Teddy visits his cousin), and Antioch College in the early 1960s (where Teddy as a senior staged a student production of *Hamlet*). Each of these places, and the events remembered about them, is vital to the psycho-logical script underneath the painstakingly vicious transcript of Teddy's case.

Hard-hitting, intensely detailed interrogation alternates with letters, dream sequences, memories, and other complemen-tary scripts, including the plays—*The Ohio State Murders* and *Hamlet*—that mother and son, respectively, at various times directed. Suzanne writes letters from backstage at rehearsals of *The Ohio State Murders* in Cleveland. Videotapes of Teddy's beating, taken by his brother David, become part of the eviden-tiary web of information, reminiscent of the film clips in *An Evening with Dead Essex*. These letters and "dream sequences" (6) summon further voices into the courtroom, contributing to the unsettling, hallucinatory effect of the play.

Woven between the dialogues relating to Teddy's trial are a half a dozen letters that Suzanne writes to officials seeking their help in combating the "racial persecution of our son" (8). As she reads these letters to Governor Wilder, a state senator, a congressman, the county manager, and even the NAACP, Suzanne is able to "void the madness and frenzy I feel" (16). Indignantly, she asks Wilder, "But why should we have to defend ourselves with letters of character when we are innocent?" (20). On the surface, Suzanne's letters seem realistic, yet they provoke a mother's surrealistic nightmare exploding into, and because of, the legal transcript. Hallucination is reality in *Sleep Deprivation Chamber*. Many of Suzanne's letters disclose, in fact, deeply intimate fragments of her life. Teddy's own lawyer accuses her of being "too emotional" (35). She ends a letter to Governor Wilder with "I keep dreaming of suffocation" (20), and to the county manager she confesses, "In the middle of that same night [as Teddy's arrest] I dreamed about men living underneath the Westside Highway at 96th Street" (7). In scene 2, just before the "pretrial deposition," she tells a senator that students "take [Patrice, her daughter] to the Quad where she is condemned to stand naked" (27), as Teddy metaphorically will be when her voice stops and the white prosecuting attorney's begins.

In several dream scenes, Suzanne recalls an event from her childhood in the 1940s when her father, an NAACP leader, and his friends met on the lake in Aurora, Ohio, singing "Let Me Call You Sweetheart." As Teddy's trial fades for just a few moments, Suzanne's father and his friends sing *very softly.* But Suzanne's recollections express more than nostalgia for a more tranquil era or the love extending from her father to her son. Her memories interrogate the trial process itself, with all of its injustice, to affirm that her father fought "to make Cleveland a better place for Negroes" (43), a powerful contrast to and antidote for the racism in Arlington in 1991. She further recalls, "I walked down a path lined with whitewashed stones. But seeing into the wooden cabin where my father and his friends sat was difficult. The Canadian Soldier moths covered the screen door of the cabin" (60). The color and animal symbolism of this dream allegory are reconfigured into harrowing warnings in Teddy's ordeal. The white stones conjure up an image of Officer Holzer "whitewashing" his testimony to cover up his actions. The Canadian Soldiers (the exaggerated insects) prevented Suzanne from seeing her father in the brown cabin (a beautiful metonymy) just as Arlington soldiers (present-day, Kafkaesque "moths") stop her from seeing her son happy and free. Suzanne's childhood symbols are transformed into contemporary comments on Teddy's ordeal.

In some of Suzanne's dream sequences, lines, characters, and scenes from *Hamlet* spring up unexpectedly at pivotal points, further disorienting audiences and increasing their fears. *Hamlet* functions as a mirror, or analogue, just as passages from Tennyson and Hardy do in *The Ohio State Murders* or the Hollywood sets do in *Movie Star*. As Suzanne dreams her *Hamlet* nightmare, Teddy lives it on stage. She puts him into the *Hamlet* of her mind. Like Hamlet, Teddy is plunged into a nightmare of political corruption, revenge, and madness. Teddy, like Shakespeare's tragic hero, is watched, questioned, slated for extinction in a police state where something is rotten. In such a world, Teddy's plight is indeed Hamlet-like for his mother. In her transformative dream sequences of *Hamlet,* Suzanne becomes a redeemed Gertrude, Teddy a threatened Hamlet, Hamlet's father's murder the basis for Teddy's search for justice, Claudius's crime is Holzer's brutality, and Arlington turns into Denmark.

In Suzanne's dream, Teddy had been directing *Hamlet* during his senior year at college when the incident took place. It is worth noting that *Sleep Deprivation Chamber* begins with the *"Student Cast sits with scripts and books . . . [in] the rehearsal hall and backstage . . . almost dark. Suzanne sits at a dressing table writing"* (5). The first words of the play, spoken by the Student Cast, allude to *Hamlet:* "Ophelia, betrayal, disillusionment," words as applicable to Hamlet's predicament as to Teddy's. Suzanne's voice then *"narrates [a] dream sequence"* in which Teddy is hung, drawn, and quartered. Following this atrocity, Suzanne reads a letter to the city manager and when she mentions that her children "were visiting their father in Arlington," she screamed as she sees Teddy. The Student Actor then reads lines from *Hamlet*'s act 1, scene 5, where the Ghost demands revenge, framing Teddy's plight in terms of Hamlet's tragedy. Through *Hamlet,* then, audiences sink deeper into the mystery in which Teddy finds himself.

Merging Elsinore and Arlington, both gone mad, Suzanne dredges up further *Hamlet* bits and pieces to express her fears. In front of a *"set of Hamlet resembling a scene from [an] Orson Welles piece"* (10), Suzanne tells Teddy she has hired a detective, and *"backstage"* writes to Virginia officials on Teddy's behalf. Intercutting scenography from the film version of *Hamlet* with her plans to help Teddy, Suzanne continues to cast her son as a tragic prince. Scene 3 begins with her juxtaposing nightmares about Teddy's defense with *Hamlet* again. "I dream Governor Wilder answers my letters. Enclosed is a thesis on the force and effect of firing all manual weapons and another thesis on present remedies against the plague and the play *Hamlet*" (41). Recalling *Hamlet* earlier, Suzanne asserts, "I offer the Policeman poison" after witnessing Teddy *"being kicked in the stomach"* (12). Shakespeare's play becomes a weapon in the arsenal of documents Suzanne relies on to aid her son. When she is most alarmed, Suzanne dreams of Teddy as Hamlet standing in Yorick's grave. Several short dream scenes with Teddy *"in Yorick's grave"* (42) are then sandwiched between interrogatories from the Unseen Questioner, symbolizing Teddy's pending doom. During Edelstein's interrogation of Holzer, *"Standing in Yorick's grave, Teddy cries out, 'Mom, help me.'"*

As *Sleep Deprivation Chamber* ends, and the judge gives her verdict, *"Yorick's grave vanishes"* (72), but not its effect. Though the judge strikes the motion to convict Teddy, she refuses "to comment on any of the rationale" for her decision, simply concluding that she wanted to "hold police officers to a higher standard" and that insufficient evidence existed to "constitute" an assault charge. Rather than charging the police for their crimes, the judge gives only a verbal reprimand when the officer deserved far greater punishment. As the play ends, Teddy, alone on the stage, watches *"the film of his beating"* and *"his screams."* The sound of those screams will be heard long after the play is over. The rest is not silence.

Motherhood 2000

Although *Motherhood 2000* was written before *Sleep Deprivation Chamber*, the events it describes occur after those of *Sleep Deprivation Chamber*, and so it is more helpful to discuss it after that play. *Motherhood 2000* is primarily a monologue spoken by Suzanne Alexander, who recalls how nine years ago a policeman brutally beat her son and how she battled the corrupt system of justice behind this action. Concerned with the aftereffects of the incident, *Motherhood 2000* discloses how Suzanne found the policeman, named Richard Fox, as well as the other officers, and how she finally achieved justice. *Motherhood 2000* was written for a festival of new plays put on at the McCarter Theatre in Princeton, New Jersey, in January 1994. According to dramaturge Janice Paran, the theme of the festival was to express the "anxieties that grip us in this waning century of progress." Although most of the plays were brief (ten to thirty minutes), producer Loretta Creco observed: "Our hope is that some of the short plays will be the start of longer works by these writers."[23] That was the case with *Motherhood 2000,* the earlier, shorter work that evolved into *Sleep Deprivation Chamber.*

Set in an apocalyptic New York City, *Motherhood 2000* bewails an America caught in urban terror. Like many creative works of the 1990s, Kennedy's play grapples with prophecies about a new millennium. It reads like a postmodern autopsy for a body of social and political evils. Gangs roam the streets, homeless people crowd everywhere, refugees pour into the city. Fights, bombs exploding, and food shortages are daily events. Even in the brownstone where Suzanne lives, it "was impossible to tell friends from enemies." Haitians, Californians, and neo-Nazis occupied different floors, and "each group had their own agenda, wars, and language" (231). National monuments become part of this landscape of terror. "City officials were constantly drowned near the Statue of Liberty" (231), and criminals sought refuge in national landmarks like the Soldiers and Sailors Monument. "Sitting on the grass" in front of this monument, she unexpectedly finds Fox playing Christ in a miracle play, joined by the other Virginia police officials who broke the law and now sought sanctuary. Fox's troupe calls themselves the Oliviers, appropriating the name of the respected British actor Sir Laurence Olivier. Ironically, Fox initially left Virginia to work for the White House and the FBI, further linking him with governmental cover-ups and misdeeds.

On the roof of her brownstone (attics and roofs always mark places of ghastly epiphanies in Kennedy's canon), Suzanne watches the troupe stage their play on the Crucifixion. Realizing that her time had come for revenge, she "decided to join their company. I had told them I had once been a playwright and had taught at Harvard [and] . . . was relieved to see they did not remember my name from my son's case" (231). They hired her, their only black member, and "said I could rewrite a section of the play." Alexander then sits on the roof rewriting that section, which she interpolates as the playlet ending *Motherhood 2000*. From her monologue flows *"the play [that] appears before her"* (232) as she moves from writing to joining the cast as one of four Roman soldiers at the Crucifixion. The mother/writer becomes a character, stage manager, and director in her own play, ingeniously layering and embedding fiction within fiction. Inscribing herself in the play, she creates a dramatic space for a hearing that will ensure justice. As in *An Evening with Dead Essex,* Kennedy uses theater as a political weapon to expose and punish a corrupt legal system, grown even more flagrant now in new-millennial New York.

As in *The Ohio State Murders* and *Sleep Deprivation Chamber,* Kennedy conflates various time frames to express the range of Suzanne's thoughts. Within her monologue, she juxtaposes memories of an earlier, kinder New York, when her son was a child eating ice cream and sightseeing, against present-day New York, "where civil unrest and chaos . . . never ceased" (231). She then moves back even further to the Crucifixion, but then fast-forwards to show the apocalyptic horrors of New York in 2000. Echoing another seemingly distant time, the embedded short play on the Crucifixion in *Motherhood 2000* is written in early modern English, reminiscent of Passion plays such as *The Wakefield Cycle* (ca. 1400). Even more politically shocking, the pristine reverence of the dialogue in the brief play contrasts with the patois of crime in a futuristic New York.

As the soldiers insult Christ with jibes and argue over his tunic in the embedded script, Kennedy assigns the last line to herself as Writer: "I spoke my lines coughing, wheezing . . . then found my place directly before Fox and struck him in the head with a hammer." "*He falls*" (233). The levels of irony are more intricate than a first reading of the play might suggest. Revealing how motherhood works in this futuristic millennium, Kennedy rewrites sacred history and its fictionalization by the Oliviers to claim a mother's right of revenge. Suzanne has thereby become both soldier and executioner. In 2000, with the legal system crumbling, mothers are transformed from weeping women at the foot of the cross into militant Marys who give their sons the justice they have earned with their blood. Suzanne thus murders a false Christ, a fugitive from her maternal law, who masquerades as the Savior. But clearly Fox is no savior; his "acting" of Christ is a ruse to evade justice as he shamelessly performs the role of deity in front of public monuments. He is miscast; he is closer to the taunting soldiers in the real Passion of Christ.

Ultimately, the irony of *Motherhood 2000* extends to Suzanne's own son. The agonies he has already suffered at the hands of Fox and his cohorts sound very much like the Roman soldiers' offenses against Christ: Fox "handcuffed my son and kicked him again and again in the stomach" (229); "my son was knocked to the ground and beaten in the head and face, kicked in the chest and stomach and dragged in the mud by a policeman" (230). Like Christ, who trumpeted the rights of the poor and enshackled, "my beloved son . . . traveled the country giving speeches for the causes of Blacks" (230). Suzanne's son is not shamming holiness on a cross like Fox but saving others in Washington, D.C., for the venerable cause of social justice, something Malcolm X worked (and died) for as well as did Suzanne's husband and Frantz Fanon.

CHAPTER 8

Lasting Reflections of Kennedy's Art

June and Jean in Concert

June and Jean in Concert premiered at the Signature Theatre in November 1995, directed by founder James Houghton, with a "musical score and songs" written by Loren Toolajian.[1] The play is an adaptation of Kennedy's *People Who Led to My Plays,* her life told through pictures and words. In bringing her autobiography to the stage, Kennedy converted her *People* scrapbook into a promptbook. Recalling intimate memories of her childhood years living in a middle-class family in Cleveland during the 1930s and 1940s, Kennedy once again functions as character, chorus, director, and author of her own life as well as a witness to it. Not only is the play a mirror of Kennedy's early family life, it is also a reflection of many of her themes, characters, and dramatic techniques. *June and Jean,* accordingly, might be treated as a crucible for Kennedy's art, a script showing us how her art evolved.

The play is peopled with fictionalized versions of Kennedy's family members. Alexis Greene observed that "*June and Jean* is a delicate memory play, a fugue for the voices of a family which, by now, exists only in Kennedy's past."[2] That fictionalized family includes Aunt Ella, a choric speaker; the father, Winston; her brother, Jackie; and her mother, Estelle. Kennedy projects herself through twin sisters, June and Jean, further reinforcing her fascination with "alter egos and divided selves."[3] As representatives of Kennedy's psyche and imagination, twins also play a major role in *The Ohio State Murders.* June and Jean, however, are individually and together Adrienne Kennedy; hence, they are "in concert" both as performers and as the playwright herself. Moreover, June and Jean might be regarded as "two sides of one person—the author as a young girl—and June's Ghost, a side that Jean, for one reason or another, kills off."[4] The history of the twins, which is the subject of *June and Jean,* transforms psychological biography into theater.

The way the stage is arranged reflects the different acting areas, or influences, these characters exert on Kennedy's memory. Clive Barnes claims that *June and Jean* "is a mood piece—dependent not simply on the poised, slightly artificial writing but also on the staging."[5] As in Kennedy's earlier, surrealistic plays like *Funnyhouse of a Negro* and *The Owl Answers,* each character speaks from a symbolic place. Aunt Ella's ghost is seated on a porch swing above the stage; later, she is joined by June's Ghost (260), both serving as female spirits of protection and inspiration, almost like guardian angels over the production. The twins are seated behind a piano downstage; June and Jean also appear there and upstage as young girls costumed in pink child's dresses, the kind Kennedy wore in an early snapshot of her that appears in *People.* "Far left, an assortment of characters appear on other levels and behind other scrims" while Dr. Mays, the president of Morehouse College, "sit[s] formally across the width of the apron."[6]

Even though *June and Jean* is not as traumatizing as *Funnyhouse of a Negro* or *A Rat's Mass,* Kennedy nevertheless still weaves a family's life sorrows—the mad Aunt Ella, her parents' divorce, June's death, and her father's as well—into the fabric of her play. Howard Kissel too narrowly asserted that "this fairly placid portrait doesn't really help us understand Kennedy's plays which are full of rage and resentment."[7] But the hurt, though softened in *June and Jean,* still comes through. Even though Kennedy resides in both sisters, it is clear that when June dies, it is her twin sister Jean who symbolizes the Adrienne who survived and wrote *Funnyhouse of a Negro, A Lesson in Dead Language,* and *A Rat's Mass.* In fact, lines from these plays are incorporated into *June and Jean,* with those from *A Rat's Mass* focusing most harrowingly on sibling relationships (257). Sharing Adrienne's/Jean's future with an audience, June provides a valuable family history that elucidates the genesis of *Funnyhouse of a Negro:* "Yet they [the parents] will divorce one spring in 1961. Suddenly that spring Jesus will become a character in the play Jean will write. . . . But this spring, sitting in the Pensione Sabrina, she will go on creating a cruel Jesus" (249). As in *Funnyhouse of a Negro, The Owl Answers, Movie Star,* and *She Talks to Beethoven,* Kennedy includes a historical figure, Dr. Mays from Morehouse College, her father's alma mater, along with her fictionalized selves and those of her family. Visiting the girls' home to discuss racial issues of the day with their father, Dr. Mays's presence further authenticates the vibrant household of ideas and frustrated dreams that Kennedy herself lived in as a child. Like Kennedy's father, Dr. Mays fought the canker of prejudice.

Psychically, however, it is Kennedy's mother who is the centerpiece for *June and Jean in Concert,* as she had been in effect for much of Kennedy's canon. Jean speaks about her mother's beauty, her hair, and her keen desire to have her daughters succeed. What she possessed "belonged to me," proudly recalls Jean. The twins' mother is the model that shaped them (and even their brother) into careful readers, and potentially famous writers. As brother Jackie remembers, "She shares her secret thoughts and tears over the movies she takes me to see. She collected photographs of her and my father's youth in Atlanta and keeps them in scrapbooks so that I am able to imagine my parents as they were when they were young" (253). Both girls revere their mother's influence on their work. Most important of all, the mother's dreams become the basis for Jean's (and Kennedy's) writing, reinforcing a key idea from *People,* as the other twin sister, June, reveals that "in the morning I can hardly wait to hear about them. The stories she tells of them are all as exciting as the movies of Frankenstein and Dracula I see at the Waldorf" (247). Similarly, Jean confesses: "The people my mother dreams about continue to grow in my imagination. Like the people in the red scrapbook, they often know each other and knew my parents when they were young. I list them in my mind as I sit on the front steps of our house" (248). The mother's dreams are provocative art, adumbrating Kennedy's tortured dreams in *Funnyhouse of a Negro, The Owl Answers,* or *A Rat's Mass.* Ironically, the mother's dreams of people are first transformed into Kennedy's earlier surrealistic plays and then into memoirs, and, finally, recaptured in this signal play from the mid-1990s.

Beyond question, the fictional mother in *June and Jean* is closely modeled after Kennedy's own mother, who, as we saw, profoundly influenced her work. In an interview with Lisa Jones, Kennedy revealed:

My mother plays a monumental role in all of this. She read parts of the Bible to me while she was making dinner. One winter she read all the Psalms. But reading to me was only part of it. My mother narrated her daily life to me. She'd tell me what happened when she went to the store, and her tale would be full of images. She could tell the most simple story cranked up a thousand decibels. She'd also tell me about her dreams and about her family in Georgia. . . . Her stories were very intense—there was a lot of anger there, sarcasm and humor. She could really describe people so brilliantly. No doubt I was a captive audience. I didn't realize it at the time but I was her only audience. My mother came from a split family. . . . She majored in drama at Atlanta University and had all these photos of herself in these dresses. We would listen to the soaps on the radio and she'd describe to me what she thought Stella Dallas or this one or that one was going through. Once every two weeks we'd go to the movies together. She named me after a movie star—Adrienne Ames. There's no doubt that she saw herself as a dramatic heroine. She would deny that if you talked to her right now, but it's clear.[8]

Kennedy's recollections about her mother—fictionalized in *June and Jean*—read like a compendium of sources for and dramatic techniques in her own works.

In 1992, director Gerald Freedman adapted *People* as a dramatic reading and brought it to thirty-five Cleveland locations, including Kennedy's mother's church, Mount Zion Congregational Church. After seeing this adaptation, Kennedy's mother, Mrs. Etta Hawkins, offered some pertinent information for understanding her daughter's works. She claimed she was worried about pushing Adrienne into a career in teaching, but admitted, "I had to finally say to her . . . forget about the school teaching, forget about what I and your daddy want for you. If you do the thing you really want to do and you give it your all, you're going to be happy."[9] That advice—to give her art her all—led Kennedy to a highly influential career writing about the people she knew, especially her mother. As we have repeatedly seen, her mother's dreams—like those Jean and June loved to hear about—indelibly shaped Kennedy's life and work. In *June and Jean,* the mother leaves a legacy of dreams that fascinated her daughters just as the horror films and romantic movies flowing through *People* captivated Kennedy.

In fact, much of Kennedy's material for *June and Jean* comes directly from the first two sections of *People*—"Elementary School" and "High School." Coupled with *People, June and Jean* gives us a clear sense of Adrienne Kennedy's past and where she has gone. Characteristic of Kennedy's earlier plays, as well as *The Ohio State Murders,* Jean, June, and Aunt Ella do not tell a linear narrative but shift back and forth in act 1 from Easter 1943 to Christmas Eve, 1942, and then in act 2 move from December 1941 forward to November 1974 and finally back to the spring of 1947. Challenging the politics of a conventional plot, the narratives in *June and Jean,* as in Kennedy's other plays, are told from a feminine perspective of recursive time, not in the rational progression of a masculine-ordered narrative.

Turning pages of a physical scrapbook—*People*—backwards and forwards, Kennedy creates the prism through which her memory is narrated. She thus filters events through her characters as they replicate in fictions what she lived in life. We learn about her Glenville neighborhood in Cleveland, her "straw hat with cherries on the brim" (242), meals, friends, games, and an Easter celebration at a church where the preacher told of the horrifying events of Good Friday, and "gilt-edged cards of Jesus that the church gave us in Sunday school [that] hypnotized me" (240), as June recollects. The family's closeness comes across through memories of Sunday drives in their father's 1937

Plymouth, the thrills of the movies, a trip to see Paul Robeson, and visits to grandparents in Montezuma, Georgia.

Harrowing moments are a part of family life, too, as when June graphically records that an ambulance came for their mother after a miscarriage: "She looked like she was dying . . . the color of her skin was almost purple" (241). We hear about June sleeping in her father's old room in Montezuma and falling to her death from the window, packing generations of tragedy into the event and then sealing the memory forever in Jean's work. Just before an "interlude," Jean records this obsequy: "We buried my twin sister three days after Easter" (250). That sacred holiday of resurrection, the one with which the play begins, evolves as the central one in *June and Jean in Concert,* suggesting that Jean's memories of her girlhood (like Kennedy's) can be reborn but only thanks to the suffering in mind and spirit that gave them birth.

Among the most important props in *June and Jean* are the books the twins, their mother, and their Aunt Ella create and bequeath, symbols looking forward and back in time to Kennedy's practice of embedding texts (from Hardy, Shakespeare, Tennyson, Beethoven, Fanon) in her plays. Key events in *June and Jean in Concert* occur around the making and keeping of books, just as the very play was made from an earlier book, *People Who Led to My Plays.* As we have seen, the power of books is both sacred and tragic throughout Kennedy's canon. Suzanne, for example, recounts the horrors of *The Ohio State Murders* standing surrounded by books in the library. As Aunt Ella points out, from their earliest years Jean and June prized their "autograph books in which they write the history of their family" (240). Books are essential to performing and preserving self, two of the most characteristic, defining elements of Kennedy's family and art in *Jean and June in Concert.*

Books are as essential to Kennedy's family album as to her theater. They provide a dense intertexuality, where books comment on and frame other books. The mother's "red scrapbook" gave Jean access into her mother's dreams, the mortar with which to build her plays. The girls savor their Sleeping Beauty books (241) and a slim book of Negro spirituals (242). Jean remembers "a room filled with theatre books" in high school (258); and June esteems "a bookcase [of] . . . old books" (243) a previous owner generously left for them. June keeps a scrapbook of her favorite pictures (248), and both girls write in diaries, symbols of their psychic journeys. Jean shares an intimate detail about Kennedy's own composing process based on "a book of Giotto prints." Walking up the road "with my grandmother to the white wooden church," she confesses that we "felt we were in a holy procession." This scene makes her think how later she would "use his colors in my stories, not realizing how I had connected the Sunday school card colors, the Georgia landscape colors and the colors of Giotto" (254–55), a memory that possibly was transformed into the antithetical, the horrifying processions in A Rat's Mass. June also has "secret books" she hopes her brother Jackie has not read, perhaps alluding to Kennedy's own "Secret Paragraphs about My Brother."

Further associating women's writing with a feminine enclave from which creation and inspiration as well as pain can spring, June's Ghost instructs her sister: "Jean, if you look in the vanity table in our room in the lower left hand drawer underneath the rose colored wallpaper that lines the drawer you will find Aunt Ella's writing. She used to bring it to me in the middle of the night" (260). Aunt Ella's writing—hidden, brought out only at night, ironically under rose wallpaper symbolic of possible but forlorn love—helps explain Kennedy's emphasis on nightly compositions about and in dreams, hysterical images, and tortured love. *The Owl Answers* is filled with such nightly flights of horrifying composition. Later, Aunt Ella recalls an image of Winston "hold[ing] clippings . . . from the pages of June and Jean's autograph books and his Metropolitan Life Insurance policies" (255), blending fiction and reality, life and death. Entering June's private world, even after her death, the father reads her diaries (255), absorbing her sacred, intimate memories. June could well have been an earlier model for Sarah or Clara from *Movie Star*.

Inseparable from the books are the performances of characters writing about the events these books contain. Many scenes in *June and Jean* are built around a character actually writing, revealing on stage a family of women/writers/historiographers, again paradoxically preparing for and yet summarizing Kennedy's literate but tortured women writers, Sarah, the two Claras, and the two Suzannes, Alexander and Sand. Though writing on stage in *June and Jean* is nostalgic, elegiac, it still helps audiences see, retrospectively, why and how it may have become so painfully tragic in *Funnyhouse of a Negro, A Lesson in Dead Language,* and *Movie Star.* The twins write in tandem about their father as the minister simultaneously acclaims his contributions to civil rights in the face of an oppressive white culture (244). On stage, too, June records memories of her girlhood, her grandmother, staying in her father's old room (252–53). Jean composes out loud as she recalls the names of family and friends from her mother's scrapbook (248). Even as her father *"clutches his daughter's diaries[,] June's Ghost writes"* (256). June's Ghost memorializes her mother's childhood as the mother stares at but does not see her, sorrowfully underscoring where that honored daughter once sat (259).

But writing in *June and Jean in Concert* (as in most Kennedy plays) becomes more than just a record. Seeing it performed, audiences can witness an actual memory in the making, which only later then turned into the play based on it. In creating *Jean and June* out of *People*, therefore, Kennedy reveals once again how her own composing evolved not in a linear, chronological way but through blending present, past, and future. Dramatizing her memories, Kennedy discloses the process by which she became a writer who (re)created herself.

Notes

Chapter 1—Introduction

1. Herbert Blau, "The American Dream in American Gothic: The Plays of Sam Shepard and Adrienne Kennedy," *Modern Drama* 27 (December 1984): 531.

2. Jennifer Dunning, "Adrienne Kennedy Decides," *New York Times,* 29 December 1977, 3:13.

3. Lois More Overbeck, "The Life of the Work: A Preliminary Sketch," in *Intersecting Boundaries: The Theatre of Adrienne Kennedy,* ed. Paul K. Bryant-Jackson and Lois More Overbeck, 13–20 (Minneapolis: University of Minnesota Press, 1992); see also Kennedy's preface to *Deadly Triplets: A Theatre Mystery and Journal* (Minneapolis: University of Minnesota Press, 1990), ix.

4. Scott T. Cummings, "Theatre: Invisible Career: Adrienne Kennedy," *Boston Phoenix,* 31 March–6 April 2000, 7.

5. Caroline Jackson Smith, "From Drama to Literature: The Unparalleled Vision of Adrienne Kennedy," *Black Masks,* August/September 1996, 15.

6. Marc Robinson, *The Other American Drama* (Cambridge: Cambridge University Press, 1994), 120.

7. Clive Barnes, "*A Rat's Mass* Weaves Drama of Poetry Fabric," *New York Times,* 1 November 1969, 24.

8. Mel Tapley, "*Funnyhouse of a Negro* Reveals America's Obsessions," *New York Amsterdam News,* 30 September 1995, 21.

9. "Because of the King of France," *Black Orpheus: A Journal of Afro-American Literature* 10 (1963): 30–37; reprinted in *The Adrienne Kennedy Reader* (Minneapolis: University of Minnesota Press, 2001), 3–6. All references to Kennedy's plays are from this edition unless otherwise noted.

10. Adrienne Kennedy, "A Growth of Images," *Drama Review* 21 (December 1977): 42.

11. Ben Brantley, "Restless Voices of a Writer's Past," *New York Times,* 13 November 1995, A1.

12. Quoted in Werner Sollors, "*People Who Led to My Plays:* Adrienne Kennedy's Autobiography," in *Intersecting Boundaries: The Theatre of Adrienne Kennedy,* ed. Paul K. Bryant-Jackson and Lois More Overbeck (Minneapolis: University of Minnesota Press, 1992), 14.

13. Smith, "From Drama to Literature," 15.

14. Elin Diamond, "An Interview with Adrienne Kennedy," *Studies in American Drama, 1945–Present* 4 (1989): 143–57; reprinted in *Speaking on Stage: Interviews with Contemporary Playwrights,* ed. Philip C. Kolin and Colby H. Kullman (Tuscaloosa: University of Alabama Press, 1996), 130. All references to Kennedy's autobiography are from *People Who Led to My Plays* (New York: Theatre Communications Group, 1987).

15. Shannon Jackson, "Staging a Scrapbook: Adrienne Kennedy's Post-Modern Art of Memory," *Theatre Annual* 46 (1993): 75.

16. William Brasmer and Dominick Peter Consolo, eds., *Black Drama; An Anthology* (Indianapolis: C. E. Merrill, 1970), 358.

17. Suzan-Lori Parks, "Adrienne Kennedy," *Bomb,* no. 5 (Winter 1996): 44.

18. Among Kennedy's papers housed at the Harry Ransom Humanities Research Center at the University of Texas at Austin are several handwritten drafts of *Pale Blue Flowers.*

19. "Secret Paragraphs about My Brother," *Grand Street* 55 (Winter 1996): 113–17; reprinted in *The Adrienne Kennedy Reader* (Minneapolis: University of Minnesota Press, 2001), 235.

20. Diamond, "Interview with Adrienne Kennedy," 137.

21. Kennedy, "Because of the King of France," 3–4.

22. Sollors, "*People Who Led to My Plays:* Adrienne Kennedy's Autobiography," 14, 20n20.

23. Scott T. Cummings, "Adrienne Kennedy," *American Theatre,* 22 June 1992, 32.

24. Cal Wilson, "Adrienne Kennedy: The Dream Experience on Stage," *Impressions: The Magazine of the Arts* 1, no. 4 (June 1976): 34.

25. Alexander Stevens, "Fear and Loathing in 'Ohio State,'" *TAB Arts & More,* 21 March 2000, 13.

26. Kathleen Betsko and Rachel Koenig, eds. "Adrienne Kennedy," in *Interviews with Contemporary American Women Playwrights* (New York: Beech Tree Books, 1987), 252.

27. Faye Sholiton, "Welcome Home, Adrienne Kennedy," *Northeast Ohio Avenues* (Cleveland), March 1992, 5.

28. Betsko and Koenig, "Adrienne Kennedy," 252.

29. Patti Hartigan, "Adrienne Kennedy Is Fragile and Ferocious," Arts Etc., *Boston Globe,* 26 March 2000, N1.

30. Parks, "Adrienne Kennedy," 44.

31. Hartigan, "Adrienne Kennedy Is Fragile," N1.

32. Paul K. Bryant-Jackson and Lois More Overbeck, "Adrienne Kennedy: An Interview," in *Intersecting Boundaries: The Theatre of Adrienne Kennedy* (Minneapolis: University of Minnesota Press, 1992), 5.

33. Zora Neale Hurston, *Dust Tracks on a Road: An Autobiography* (1942), ed. Robert E. Hemenway, 2nd ed. (Urbana: University of Illinois Press, 1984), 213.

34. Hartigan, "Adrienne Kennedy Is Fragile," N1.

35. Bryant-Jackson and Overbeck, "Adrienne Kennedy: An Interview," 12.

36. Betsko and Koenig, "Adrienne Kennedy," 249.

37. Ibid.

38. Stevens, "Fear and Loathing," 13.

39. W. E. B. DuBois, *The Souls of Black Folk,* quoted in *Understanding Literature,* ed. Walter Kalaidjian, Judith Roof, and Stephen Watt (Boston: Houghton Mifflin, 2004), 964.

40. Parks, "Adrienne Kennedy," 44.

41. Helene Keyssar, *Feminist Theatre: An Introduction to the Plays of Contemporary British and American Women* (London: Macmillan, 1984), 109.

42. Kennedy, "Growth of Images," 44.

43. Werner Sollors, "Owls and Rats in the American Funnyhouse: Adrienne Kennedy's Drama," *American Literature* 63 (September 1991): 518.

44. For information on film noir in this paragraph, I am indebted to Bernard F. Dick, *Anatomy of Film* (New York: Bedford/St. Martin's, 2002), 139–44, here 140.

45. Kennedy, "Growth of Images," 44.

46. Yahoo! Health, "Dissociative Identity Disorder (Multiple Personality Disorder)," http://health.yahoo.com/centers/personality/96408437.html (accessed 5 February 2004). Originally published by *Psychology Today.*

47. Ibid.

48. Sidran Foundation, "About Trauma—Dissociative Disorders," http://www.sidran.org/didbr.html (accessed 29 January 2004).

49. Edith Oliver, "Theatre," *New Yorker,* 25 June 1969, 77.

50. Diamond, "An Interview with Adrienne Kennedy," 137.

51. Betsko and Koenig, "Adrienne Kennedy," 254.

52. Robinson, *Other American Drama,* 124.

Chapter 2—A War of Selves in *Funnyhouse of a Negro*

1. Adrienne Kennedy, "Becoming a Playwright," *American Theatre* 4 (February 1988): 26–27.

2. The critics, respectively, are Howard Taubman, "Adrienne Kennedy Play Opens at East End," *New York Times,* 15 January 1964, 25; and Edith Oliver, "The Theatre: Off-Broadway," *New Yorker,* 25 January 1964, 78.

3. Kennedy, "Growth of Images," 47.

4. Taubman, "Kennedy Play Opens," 25.

5. Adrienne Kennedy, "On the Writing of *Funnyhouse*," in *The Adrienne Kennedy Reader,* ed. Werner Sollors (Minneapolis: University of Minnesota Press, 2001), 27.

6. Susan E. Meigs, "No Place But the Funnyhouse: The Struggle for Identity in Three Kennedy Plays," in *Modern American Drama: The Female Canon,* ed. June Schlueter (Rutherford, N.J.: Fairleigh Dickinson University Press, 1990), 174.

7. Sollors, "Owls and Rats," 517.

8. Blau, "American Dream," 531.

9. Frantz Fanon, *Black Skin, White Masks* (New York: Grove Press, 1967).

10. Keyssar, *Feminist Theatre,* 111.

11. Philip C. Kolin, "From the Zoo to the Funnyhouse: A Comparison of Edward Albee's *Zoo Story* with Adrienne Kennedy's *Funnyhouse of a Negro*," *Theatre Southwest,* April 1989, 8–16.

12. Robert Tener, "Theatre of Identity: Adrienne Kennedy's Portrait of the Black Woman," *Studies in Black Literature* 6 (Summer 1975): 3.

13. Kennedy, "On the Writing of *Funnyhouse*," 27.

14. Kennedy, "Growth of Images," 42.

15. Joseph Pearce, "Edith Sitwell," CatholicAuthors.com, http://www.catholicauthors.com/sitwell.html (accessed 3 April 2004).

16. These views have been expressed, respectively, by Leonard Greene, "'Funny House' Sees Sad Aspects of Race," *New York University Washington Square News,* 28 November 1984, 5; Margit Sichert, "The Staging of Excessive Emotions: Adrienne Kennedy's *Funnyhouse of a Negro*," *REAL: The Yearbook of Research in English and American Literature* 16 (2000): 229–51; and Fred Tapley, "*Funnyhouse of a Negro* Reveals America's Obsession," *New York Amsterdam News,* 30 September 1995, 21.

17. Matthew C. Roudané, "Dreamglides: The Theatre of Adrienne Kennedy," in *American Drama since 1960* (New York: Twayne Publishers, 1996), 78.

18. Karen D'Souza, "Reflections of Racism's Power to Distort," *San Jose Mercury News,* 27 May 2000, 11E.

19. Quoted in Sichert, "Staging," 231.

20. Erin Hurley, "Blackout: Utopian Technologies in Adrienne Kennedy's *Funnyhouse of a Negro,*" *Modern Drama* 47 (Summer 2004): 209.

21. Blau, "American Dream," 533.

22. Susan Sontag, "Going to the Theatre," *Partisan Review* 31 (Spring 1964): 293.

23. Bryant-Jackson and Overbeck, "Adrienne Kennedy: An Interview," 3–4.

24. Sichert, "Staging," 243.

25. Sollors, "Owls and Rats," 509.

26. Quoted in Greene, "'Funny House' Sees Sad Aspects of Race," 5.

27. See Blau, "American Dream"; and Jacqueline Wood, "Weight of the Mask: Parody and the Heritage of Minstrelsy in Adrienne Kennedy's *Funnyhouse of a Negro,*" *Journal of Dramatic Theory and Criticism* 17 (Spring 2003): 5–24.

28. Sichert, "Staging," 242.

29. Margaret B. Wilkerson, "Diverse Angels of Vision: Two Black Women Playwrights," in *Intersecting Boundaries: The Theatre of Adrienne Kennedy,* ed. Paul K. Bryant-Jackson and Lois More Overbeck (Minneapolis: University of Minnesota Press, 1992), 73.

30. Wood, "Weight of the Mask," 17.

31. Susan Gubar, *White Skin, Black Face in American Culture* (New York: Oxford University Press, 1997), 77–80.

32. Jochen Achilles "African American Drama," in *English Literatures in International Contexts,* ed. Heinz Antor and Klaus Stierstorfer (Heidelberg: C. Winter, 2000), 208; and Wilkerson, "Diverse Angels," 73.

33. Robert Scanlon, "Surrealism as Mimesis," in *Intersecting Boundaries: The Theatre of Adrienne Kennedy,* ed. Paul K.

Bryant-Jackson and Lois More Overbeck (Minneapolis: University of Minnesota Press, 1992), 101.

34. Meigs, "No Place," 174.

35. Ben Brantley, "Glimpsing Solitude in Worlds Black and White," *New York Times,* 25 September 1995, C11.

36. Sollors, "Owls and Rats," 519.

37. Overbeck, "Life of the Work," 26.

38. Michael Billington, "A Racial Dilemma," *Times* (London), 29 April 1968, 37.

39. Eric Shorter, "Royal Court's Latest Victoria is Negro," *Daily Telegraph* (London), 29 April 1968, 17.

40. Margo Jefferson, "A Family's Story Merges with the Nation's," *New York Times,* 8 October 1995, 2:43.

Chapter 3—*Cities in Bezique*

1. Adrienne Kennedy, *Cities in Bezique: Two One-Act Plays* (New York: Samuel French, 1969.) References to *The Owl Answers* are from *The Adrienne Kennedy Reader;* references to *A Beast Story* are from *Cities in Bezique.*

2. Wolfgang Binder, "A MELUS Interview: Adrienne Kennedy," *MELUS: The Journal of the Society for the Study of the Multi-Ethnic Literature of the United States* 12, no. 3 (Fall 1985): 104.

3. Ibid.

4. Paul Carter Harrison, ed., *Kuntu Drama: Plays of the African Continuum* (New York: Grove Press, 1974), 191–202.

5. Kimberly W. Benston, "*Cities in Bezique:* Adrienne Kennedy's Expressionistic Vision," *CLA Journal* 20 (December 1976): 241.

6. BBC Homepage, "Bezique—The Card Game," http://www.bbc.co.uk/hzgz/guide/A646724 (accessed 1 May 2004).

7. Elin Diamond, "Mimesis in Syncopated Time: Reading Adrienne Kennedy," in *Intersecting Boundaries: The Theatre of*

Adrienne Kennedy, ed. Paul K. Bryant-Jackson and Lois More Overbeck (Minneapolis: University of Minnesota Press, 1992), 134.

8. Benston, "*Cities in Bezique,*" 235.

9. E. Barnsley Brown, "Passed Over: The Tragic Mulatta and Integration of Identity in Adrienne Kennedy's Plays," *African American Review* 35 (Summer 2001): 289.

10. Benston, "*Cities in Bezique,*" 239.

11. Goodman Theatre (Chicago), *Transformations* [including *The Owl Answers*], theater program, 1997.

12. Walter Kerr, "Walter Kerr on *Cities in Bezique:* Some Day Adrienne Kennedy Will . . . ," *New York Times,* 19 January 1969, 2:3.

13. Richard P. Cooke, "The Theater: World of Fantasy," *Wall Street Journal,* 14 January 1969, 18.

14. Kennedy, "Growth of Images," 45.

15. Binder, "MELUS Interview," 107.

16. Clive Barnes, "Theatre: 'Cities in Bezique' Arrives at the Public," *New York Times,* 13 January 1969, L26.

17. Carla J. McDonough, "God and the Owls: The Sacred and the Profane in Adrienne Kennedy's *The Owl Answers,*" *Modern Drama* 40 (Fall 1997): 389.

18. Jeanie Forte, "Realism, Narrative, and the Feminist Playwright—A Problem of Reception," *Modern Drama* 32 (1989): 115–27, here 121.

19. McDonough, "God and the Owls," 391.

20. Rosemary Curb, "(Hetero)Sexual Terrors in Adrienne Kennedy's Early Plays," in *Intersecting Boundaries: The Theatre of Adrienne Kennedy,* ed. Paul K. Bryant-Jackson and Lois More Overbeck (Minneapolis: University of Minnesota Press, 1992), 151.

21. Susan Booth, "*The Owl Answers,*" in *Transformations,* Goodman Theatre (Chicago), theater program, 1997.

22. Betsko and Koenig, "Adrienne Kennedy," 255.

23. Robinson, *Other American Drama,* 138.

24. Diamond, "Mimesis," 136.

25. McDonough, "God and the Owls," 392.

26. Tener, "Theatre of Identity," 3.

27. Barnes, "Theatre: 'Cities in Bezique,'" L26.

28. Robinson, *Other American Drama,* 138.

29. Curb, "(Hetero)Sexual Terrors," 144.

30. Chezia Thompson-Coger, "In One Act," *Sage* 7, no. 2 (Fall 1990): 65.

31. Robinson, *Other American Drama,* 133.

32. Tener, "Theatre of Identity," 2.

33. Ibid.

34. Sollors, "Owls and Rats," 522.

35. Tener, "Theatre of Identity," 2.

36. Ibid.

37. Curb, "(Hetero)Sexual Terrors," 145.

38. Brown, "Passed Over," 291.

39. Quoted in Hartigan, "Adrienne Kennedy Is Fragile," N2.

40. Benston, "*Cities in Bezique,*" 240.

41. Robinson, *Other American Drama,* 138.

42. Tennessee Williams, *Dragon Country: A Book of Plays* (New York: New Directions, 1970).

43. Cooke, "Theatre: World of Fantasy," 18.

Chapter 4—Black Rats and White Dogs

1. Kennedy, "Growth of Images," 44.

2. Jeanie Forte, "Kennedy's Body Politic: The Mulatta, Menses, and the Medusa," in *Intersecting Boundaries: The Theatre of Adrienne Kennedy,* ed. Paul K. Bryant-Jackson and Lois More Overbeck (Minneapolis: University of Minnesota Press, 1992), 158–59.

3. Kennedy, "Growth of Images," 45.

4. Arthur Sainer, "The Theatre: *A Rat's Mass,*" *Village Voice,* 25 September 1969, 42.

5. Claudia Barnett, "'This Fundamental Challenge to Identity': Reproduction and Representation in the Drama of Adrienne Kennedy," *Theatre Journal* 48 (May 1996): 145.

6. Rosemary Curb, "'Lesson I Bleed': Adrienne Kennedy's Blood Rites," in *Women in American Theatre,* ed. Helen Krich Chinoy and Linda Walsh Jenkins (New York: Crown, 1981), 54.

7. Elinor Fuchs, "Adrienne Kennedy and the First Avant-Garde," in *Intersecting Boundaries: The Theatre of Adrienne Kennedy,* ed. Paul K. Bryant-Jackson and Lois More Overbeck (Minneapolis: University of Minnesota Press, 1992), 80.

8. Roudané, "Dreamglides," 78–79.

9. Clive Barnes, "*A Rat's Mass* Weaves Drama of Poetic Fabric," *New York Times,* 1 November 1969, 39; see also Overbeck, "Life of the Work," 30.

10. Marilyn Stasio, "The Theatre: *A Rat's Mass,*" *Cue,* 4 October 1969, 16.

11. Evita M. Castine, "Theatre Review: A Rat's Mass," *Geechi Magazine* 1, http://www.geechi.com/Rat%27sMass.htm (accessed 11 January 2003).

12. Irving Wardle, "Tormented Fury," *Times* (London), 27 May 1970, 14.

13. Curb, "(Hetero)Sexual Terrors," 146.

14. Adrienne Kennedy, quoted in "Adrienne Kennedy Decides that the Classroom Is the Thing," *New York Times,* 9 December 1977, C1.

15. Curb, "(Hetero)Sexual Terrors," 150.

16. Barnett, "This Fundamental Challenge," 147.

17. Ibid.

18. William Inge, *Four Plays by William Inge* (New York: Random House, 1958), 68–69.

19. See Philip C. Kolin and Maureen Curley, "Adrienne Kennedy's *A Lesson in Dead Language,*" *Explicator* 60 (Spring 2002): 170.

20. Robinson, *Other American Drama,* 142.

21. Howard Stein, "An Interview with Gaby Rodgers," in *Intersecting Boundaries: The Theatre of Adrienne Kennedy,* ed. Paul K. Bryant-Jackson and Lois More Overbeck (Minneapolis: University of Minnesota Press, 1992), 200.

22. Curb, "Lesson I Bleed," 51.

23. Brown, "Passed Over," 286.

24. George Ferguson, *Signs and Symbols of Christian Art* (New York: Oxford University Press, 1961), 33.

25. Anna Chupa, "St. Joseph Altars," http:www.irc.msstate .edu/~achupa/stjo/sj-stand.html (accessed 10 September 2001).

26. Suzanne Sand in *Deadly Triplets* finds "a child's white organdy dress" in an old trunk "lined with the rotting remains of wallpaper" and observes, "when I picked up the child's dress [I was] wondering had it been mine" (19). As in *A Lesson in Dead Language,* a white organdy dress here also symbolizes lost or stolen youth.

27. Kolin and Curley, "Kennedy's *Lesson,*" 171.

28. Brown, "Passed Over," 285.

Chapter 5—Acting White

1. Clive Barnes, "Back to the Future," *New York Post,* 9 July 2000, 27.

2. John Heilpern, "A Feverish Night at the Theater: Out-of-This-World Dramas," *New York Observer,* 2 October 1995, 25.

3. David Willinger, "*Funnyhouse of a Negro* and *A Movie Star Has to Star in Black and White,*" *Theatre Journal* 48 (May 1996): 223.

4. Jefferson, "Family's Story," 2:43.

5. Heilpern, "Feverish Night," 25.

6. Elin Diamond, "Rethinking Identification: Kennedy, Freud, Brecht," *Kenyon Review* 44 (Spring 1993): 96.

7. Heilpern, "Feverish Night," 25.

8. E. Barnsley Brown, "The Clash of Verbal and Visual (Con)Text: Adrienne Kennedy's (Re)Construction of Racial Polarities in *An Evening with Dead Essex* and *A Movie Star Has to Star in Black and White*," in *Hollywood on Stage: Playwrights Evaluate the Culture Industry,* ed. Kimball King (New York: Garland, 1997), 193–201.

9. Raoul Abdul, "Luminaries Honor Adrienne Kennedy at Joe Papp's," *New York Amsterdam News,* 23 September 1995, 27.

10. Diamond, "Rethinking Identification," 95.

11. See Marsha Orgeron, "Making It in Hollywood: Clara Bow, Fandom, and Consumer Culture," *Cinema Journal* 42 (Summer 2003): 76–96.

12. For a history of this stereotyping and the NAACP's protests against it, see Donald Bogle, *Toms, Coons, Mulattoes, Mammies, and Bucks: An Interpretive History of Blacks in American Film* (1973; reprint, New York: Continuum, 2001).

13. *Monica in Black and White,* produced by Fenton Bailey and Randy Barbato for HBO. Filmed at New York's Cooper Union, 3 March 2002.

14. See Linda Kintz, "The Sanitized Spectacle: What's Birth Got to Do with It? Adrienne Kennedy's *A Movie Star Has to Star in Black and White*," *Theatre Journal* 44 (March 1992): 67–86.

15. Deborah R. Geis, "A Spectator Watching My Life: Adrienne Kennedy's *A Movie Star Has to Star in Black and White*," in *Intersecting Boundaries,* ed. Paul K. Bryant-Jackson and Lois More Overbeck (Minneapolis: University of Minnesota Press, 1992), 175.

16. Michael Sommers, "Underrated Playwright Acts Dramatic Hearing," *Philadelphia Star-Ledger*, 27 September 1995.

17. Brown, "Clash of Verbal and Visual," 201.

18. Diamond, "Rethinking Identification," 90.

19. Brown, "Clash of Verbal and Visual," 198.

20. Geis, "Spectator," 173.

21. Diamond, "Rethinking Identification," 90.

22. Willinger, "*Funnyhouse* and *Movie Star*," 222.

23. Robinson, *Other American Drama,* 142.

24. Geis, "Spectator," 176–77.

25. Howard Kissel, "Plays' Mind-set Is Way Too Brainy: *Funnyhouse* and *Movie Star* Aim for the Head, but Don't Touch the Heart," *New York Daily News*, 29 September 1995, 39.

26. Geis, "Spectator," 177.

27. Brown, "Clash of Verbal and Visual," 201.

28. Robinson, *Other American Drama,* 141.

Chapter 6—*The Alexander Plays*

1. Overbeck, "Life of the Work," 37.

2. For a discussion of these techniques in film, see Julia Leyda, "Black-Audience Westerns and the Politics of Cultural Identification in the 1930s," *Cinema Journal* 42 (Fall 2002): 46–70.

3. Alisa Solomon, "Introduction," in *The Alexander Plays* (Minneapolis: University of Minnesota Press, 1992), xvi.

4. See Philip C. Kolin, "Color Connections in Adrienne Kennedy's *She Talks to Beethoven*," *Notes on Contemporary Literature* 24 (March 1994): 4–6.

5. Overbeck, "Life of the Work," 47.

6. Christopher Jones, "Ohio State Murders," *Variety,* 16 March 1992, 68.

7. Gerald Freedman, "From the Director's Notebook," in *Spotlight: Great Lakes Theater Festival,* theater program, 5–22 March 1992, 25.

8. Erin Weinberger, "Murder, Racism at Ohio State U. Explored in Alum's Play," *Ohio State University Lantern*, 31 October 2000, 7.

9. Alvin Klein, "Yale Repertory's Winterfest: A Terrific Showcase," Theatre, *New York Times,* 27 January 1991, H36.

10. Weinberger, "Murder, Racism," 7.

11. Jennifer Waters, "Standing on the Edge of the Oval," *Ohio Writer* 4 (September/October 1990): 10.

12. Marianne Evett, "Playwright's Career Crests on GLTG's Stage," *Cleveland Plain Dealer*, 11 March 1992, H8.

13. Nicole R. King, "The Alexander Plays," *Theatre Journal* 45 (October 1993): 407.

14. Michael Grossberg, "'Murders' Attacks Racism but Fails as Drama," *Columbus (Ohio) Dispatch,* 11 March 1992, 8C.

15. Quoted in Margaret Lynch, "Haunting New Play, 'Ohio State Murders,' Marks Homecoming for Adrienne Kennedy, Ruby Dee," *Spotlight: Great Lakes Theatre Festival* 6, no. 2 (February 1992): 3.

16. Quoted in Lynch, "Haunting New Play," 3.

17. Paula Maggio, "Uncovering the Layers of Darkness in *Ohio State Murders,*" Entertainment, *Cleveland City Reports*, 19 March 1992, 5.

18. Rosemary Curb, "De-Eroticizing Violence," *Belles Lettres,* Summer 1993, 50.

19. Jeff Hedrich, "Ohio State Murders: Pass Fail," Theatre, *Cleveland Edition,* 19 March 1992, 13.

20. Keith A. Joseph, "Great Lakes Theater Festival: The Shock of the New," *Cleveland Scene* 23, no. 11 (12–18 March 1992), 5.

21. David Kornhaber, "Murder in the Academy," *Harvard Crimson Online* (14 April 2000), www.thecrimson.harvard.edu/article.aspx?ref=100509 (accessed 4 February 2003).

22. Hedrich, "Ohio State Murders," 13.

23. Ibid.

Chapter 7—Kennedy's Political Morality Plays

1. Werner Sollors, "Introduction," in *Adrienne Kennedy Reader,* ed. Werner Sollors (Minneapolis: University of Minnesota Press, 2001), xi.

2. The Official Web Site of Malcolm X, "About Malcolm X: Biography," http://www.cmgww.com/historic/malcolm/about/bio.htm (accessed 10 March 2004).

3. *Malcolm X: Death of a Prophet,* directed by Woodie King (Dallas: Reel Media International, 1981).

4. William R. Elwood, "Adrienne Kennedy through the Lens of German Expressionism," in *Intersecting Boundaries: The Theatre of Adrienne Kennedy,* ed. Paul K. Bryant-Jackson and Lois More Overbeck (Minneapolis: University of Minnesota Press, 1992), 92n6.

5. See Lisa Jones, "Beyond the Funnyhouse: A Conversation with Playwright Adrienne Kennedy," *Village Voice,* 16 April 1996, 40; Robert Koehler, "Her 'Kingdom' Cometh," *Los Angeles Times,* 19 June 1993, F12; and Olga Barrios, "From Seeking One's Voice to Uttering the Scream: The Pioneering Journey of African American Women Playwrights through the 1960s and 1970s," *African American Review* 37, no. 4 (2003): 611–28.

6. Elwood, "Kennedy through the Lens," 89.

7. *Malcolm X: Death of a Prophet.*

8. Ibid.

9. Diamond, "Interview with Adrienne Kennedy," 156.

10. Frank Kryza, "An Evening with Dead Essex," *Plainville (Conn.) News,* 13 March 1974, 7.

11. Stein, "Interview with Gaby Rodgers," 202.

12. Toby Silverman Zinman, "'In the Presence of Mine Enemies': Adrienne Kennedy's *An Evening with Dead Essex,*" *Studies in American Drama, 1945–Present* 6 (1991), 4.

13. Francis Levy, "Theatre Afield," *Village Voice,* 20 March 1974, 75.

14. Mel Gussow, "Double Bill in New Haven," *New York Times,* 18 March 1974, 42.

15. Robert Vorlicky, "*Sleep Deprivation Chamber,*" *Theatre Journal* 49, no. 1 (1997): 69.

16. Lisa Jones, "Beyond the Funnyhouse," 42.

17. See Kenneth Meeks, *Driving While Black . . . How to Fight Back If You Are a Victim of Racial Profiling* (New York: Broadway Books, 2000); Sophia A. Nelson and Brian W. Jones, "Racial Profiling Is Bad Policing," *Wall Street Journal,* 2 June 1999, A12;

and Jeffrey Prescott, "New Facts on Racial Profiling," *Christian Science Monitor,* 10 May 2000, 8.

18. Bryant-Jackson and Overbeck, "Adrienne Kennedy: An Interview," 7.

19. All quotations are cited from *Sleep Deprivation Chamber* (New York: Theatre Communications Group, 1996).

20. Bridget Botelho, "*Sleep Deprivation* Awakens," *Style: The Northeastern News*, 8 November 2000, 15.

21. Ben Brantley, "Righting a Wrong in a World Out of Joint," *New York Times,* 27 February 1996, C15.

22. Ibid.

23. McCarter Theatre, *Winterfest,* theater program, January 1994.

Chapter 8—Lasting Reflections of Kennedy's Art

1. "Hum This Music 'Scores Big' with World Premiere: Composer and Musical Director Loren Toolajian Creates Magic in 'June and Jean in Concert,'" *Armenian Reporter,* 29 no. 10 (9 December 1995), 10.

2. Alexis Greene, "*June and Jean in Concert,*" *Theater-Week,* 4 December 1995, 10.

3. Ben Brantley, "Restless Voices of a Writer's Past," *New York Times,* 13 November 1995, A21, 24.

4. Greene, "*June and Jean in Concert,*" 11.

5. Clive Barnes, "Cries and Whispers," *New York Post,* 14 November 1995, 44.

6. Greene, "*June and Jean in Concert,*" 11.

7. Howard Kissel, "'June' Not Bustin' Out All Over," *New York Daily News*, 14 November 1995, 44.

8. Lisa Jones, "Beyond the Funnyhouse," 40.

9. Quoted in Margaret Bernstein, "Play Evokes Scrapbook of Memories," Commentary, *Cleveland Plain Dealer*, 2 March 1992, 1B.

Selected Bibliography

Primary Works

Plays

Adrienne Kennedy in One Act. Emergent Literatures Series. Minneapolis: University of Minnesota Press, 1988. Includes *Funnyhouse of a Negro; The Owl Answers; A Lesson in Dead Language; A Rat's Mass; Sun: A Poem for Malcolm X Inspired by His Murder; A Movie Star Has to Star in Black and White;* and adaptations of *Electra* and *Orestes.*

The Adrienne Kennedy Reader. Edited by Werner Sollors. Minneapolis: University of Minnesota Press, 2001. Includes "Because of the King of France"; *Funnyhouse of a Negro; The Owl Answers; A Lesson in Dead Language; A Rat's Mass; Sun: A Poem for Malcolm X Inspired by His Murder; A Movie Star Has to Star in Black and White;* adaptations of *Electra* and *Orestes; An Evening with Dead Essex; The Alexander Plays: She Talks to Beethoven, The Ohio State Murders, The Film Club, Dramatic Circle;* "Letter to My Students on My Sixty-first Birthday by Suzanne Alexander"; *Motherhood 2000;* "Secret Paragraphs about My Brother"; *Jean and June in Concert (Concert of Their Lives); A Letter to Flowers; Sisters Etta and Ella; Grendel and Grendel's Mother.*

The Alexander Plays. Emergent Literatures Series. Minneapolis: University of Minnesota Press, 1992.

Cities in Bezique: Two One-Act Plays. New York: Samuel French, 1969. Includes *The Owl Answers; A Beast Story.*

The Lennon Play: In His Own Write. In collaboration with John Lennon and Victor Spinetti. New York: Simon and Schuster, 1968. Adaptation of the writings of John Lennon from Lennon's *In His Own Write* and *A Spaniard in the Works.*

Sleep Deprivation Chamber. With Adam Kennedy. New York: Theatre Communication Group, 1996.

Novel

Deadly Triplets: A Theatre Mystery and Journal. Emergent Literatures Series. Minneapolis: University of Minnesota Press, 1990.

Autobiography

People Who Led to My Plays. New York: Knopf, 1987.

Interviews

Betsko, Kathleen, and Rachel Koenig, eds. "Adrienne Kennedy." In *Interviews with Contemporary Women Playwrights,* 246–58. New York: Beech Tree Books, 1987.

Binder, Wolfgang. "A MELUS Interview: Adrienne Kennedy." *MELUS: The Journal of the Society for the Study of the Multi-Ethnic Literature of the United States* 12 (Fall 1985): 99–108.

Bryant-Jackson, Paul K., and Lois More Overbeck. "Adrienne Kennedy: An Interview." In *Intersecting Boundaries: The Theatre of Adrienne Kennedy,* edited by Paul K. Bryant-Jackson and Lois More Overbeck, 3–12. Minneapolis: University of Minnesota Press, 1992.

Diamond, Elin. "An Interview with Adrienne Kennedy." In *Studies in American Drama, 1945–Present* 4 (1989): 143–57. Reprinted in *Speaking on Stage: Interviews with Contemporary American Playwrights,* edited by Philip C. Kolin and Colby H. Kullman, 125–37. Tuscaloosa: University of Alabama Press, 1996.

Hartigan, Patti. "Adrienne Kennedy Is Fragile and Ferocious." Arts Etc., *Boston Globe,* 26 March 2000, N1.

Parks, Suzan-Lori. "Adrienne Kennedy." *Bomb* 5 (Winter 1996): 42–45.

Wilson, Cal. "Adrienne Kennedy: The Dream Experience on Stage." *Impressions: Magazine of the Arts* 1 (June 1976): 34–36.

Secondary Works

Barnett, Claudia. "'This Fundamental Challenge to Identity': Reproduction and Representation in the Drama of Adrienne Kennedy." *Theatre Journal* 48 (May 1996): 141–55.

Barrios, Olga. "From Seeking One's Voice to Uttering the Scream: The Pioneeering Journey of African American Women Playwrights through the 1960s and 1970s." *African American Review* 37, no. 4 (2003): 611–28.

Benston, Kimberly W. "*Cities in Bezique:* Adrienne Kennedy's Expressionistic Vision." *CLA Journal* 20 (December 1976): 235–44.

Blau, Herbert. "The American Dream in the American Gothic: The Plays of Sam Shepard and Adrienne Kennedy." *Modern Drama* 27 (December 1984): 520–39.

Brown, E. Barnsley. "The Clash of Verbal and Visual (Con)Texts: Adrienne Kennedy's (Re)Construction of Racial Polarities in *An Evening with Dead Essex* and *A Movie Star Has to Star in Black and White.*" In *Hollywood on Stage: Playwrights Evaluate the Culture Industry,* edited and with an introduction by Kimball King, 193–201. New York: Garland, 1997.

Brown, Lorraine A. "'For the Characters Are Myself': Adrienne Kennedy's *Funnyhouse of a Negro.*" *Negro American Literature Forum* 9 (September 1975): 86–88.

Bryant-Jackson, Paul K. "Kennedy's Travelers in the American and African Continuum." In *Intersecting Boundaries: The Theatre of Adrienne Kennedy,* edited by Paul K. Bryant-Jackson and Lois More Overbeck, 45–57. Minneapolis: University of Minnesota Press, 1992.

Bryant-Jackson, Paul K., and Lois More Overbeck, eds. *Intersecting Boundaries: The Theatre of Adrienne Kennedy.* Minneapolis: University of Minnesota Press, 1992.

Curb, Rosemary. "Fragmented Selves in Adrienne Kennedy's *Funnyhouse of a Negro* and *The Owl Answers.*" *Theatre Journal* 32 (May 1980): 180–95.

———. "(Hetero)Sexual Terrors in Adrienne Kennedy's Early Plays." In *Intersecting Boundaries: The Theatre of Adrienne Kennedy,* edited by Paul K. Bryant-Jackson and Lois More Overbeck, 142–56. Minneapolis: University of Minnesota Press, 1992.

———. "'Lesson I Bleed': Adrienne Kennedy's Blood Rites." In *Women in American Theatre,* edited by Helen Krich Chinoy and

Linda Walsh Jenkins, 50–57. New York: Crown, 1981; reprint, New York: Theatre Communications Group, 1987.

———. "Re/cognition, Re/presentation, Re/creation in Woman-Conscious Drama: The Seer, the Seen, the Scene, the Obscene." *Theatre Journal* 37 (October 1985): 302–16.

Forte, Jeanie. "Kennedy's Body Politic: The Mulatta, Menses, and the Medusa." In *Intersecting Boundaries: The Theatre of Adrienne Kennedy,* edited by Paul K. Bryant-Jackson and Lois More Overbeck, 157–69. Minneapolis: University of Minnesota Press, 1992.

Geis, Deborah. "'A Spectator Watching My Life': Adrienne Kennedy's *A Movie Star Has to Star in Black and White.*" In *Intersecting Boundaries: The Theatre of Adrienne Kennedy,* edited by Paul K. Bryant-Jackson and Lois More Overbeck, 170–78. Minneapolis: University of Minnesota Press, 1992.

Hurley, Erin. "Blackout: Utopian Technologies in Adrienne Kennedy's *Funnyhouse of a Negro.*" *Modern Drama* 47 (Summer 2004): 200–218.

Jackson, Shannon. "Staging a Scrapbook: Adrienne Kennedy's Post-Modern Art of Memory." *Theatre Annual* 46 (1993): 73–83.

Kintz, Linda. "The Sanitized Spectacle: What's Birth Got to Do with It? Adrienne Kennedy's *A Movie Star Has to Star in Black and White.*" *Theatre Journal* 44 (March 1992): 67–86.

Kolin, Philip C. "From the Zoo to the Funnyhouse: A Comparison of Edward Albee's *The Zoo Story* with Adrienne Kennedy's *Funnyhouse of a Negro.*" *Theatre Southwest,* April 1989, 8–16.

———. "Orpheus Ascending: Music, Race, and Gender in Adrienne Kennedy's *She Talks to Beethoven.*" *African American Review* 28 (Summer 1994): 293–304.

Kolin, Philip C., and Maureen Curley. "A Classified Adrienne Kennedy Bibliography." *Bulletin of Bibliography* 59 (June 2002): 41–58.

McDonough, Carla J. "God and the Owls: The Sacred and the Profane in Adrienne Kennedy's *The Owl Answers.*" *Modern Drama* 40 (Fall 1997): 385–402.

Meigs, Susan E. "No Place but the Funnyhouse: The Struggle for Identity in Three Adrienne Kennedy Plays." In *Modern American Drama: The Female Canon,* edited by June Schlueter, 172–83. Rutherford, N.J.: Fairleigh Dickinson University Press, 1990.

Overbeck, Lois More. "The Life of the Work: A Preliminary Sketch." In *Intersecting Boundaries: The Theatre of Adrienne Kennedy,* edited by Paul K. Bryant-Jackson and Lois More Overbeck, 21–41. Minneapolis: University of Minnesota Press, 1992.

Robinson, Marc. "Adrienne Kennedy." In *The Other American Drama,* 115–49. Cambridge: Cambridge University Press, 1994.

Roudané, Matthew C. "Dreamglides: The Theatre of Adrienne Kennedy." In *American Drama since 1960: A Critical History,* 76–85. New York: Twayne Publishers, 1996.

Sichert, Margit. "The Staging of Excessive Emotions: Adrienne Kennedy's *Funnyhouse of a Negro.*" *The Yearbook of Research in English and American Literature* 16 (2000): 229–51.

Smith, Caroline Jackson. "From Drama to Literature: The Unparalleled Vision of Adrienne Kennedy." *Black Masks,* August/September 1996, 5–6, 14–15.

Sollors, Werner. "Owls and Rats in the American Funnyhouse: Adrienne Kennedy's Drama." *American Literature* 63 (September 1991): 507–34.

Tener, Robert L. "Theatre of Identity: Adrienne Kennedy's Portrait of the Black Woman." *Studies in Black Literature* 6 (Summer 1975): 1–5.

Zinman, Toby Silverman. "'In the Presence of Mine Enemies': Adrienne Kennedy's *An Evening with Dead Essex.*" *Studies in American Drama, 1945–Present* 6 (1991): 3–13.

Index